AGINCOURT
1415

To Bison,
Enjoy the journey! With my best wishes
Mike

AGINCOURT
1415

BATTLEFIELD GUIDE

MICHAEL K. JONES

FOREWORD
MATTHEW STRICKLAND

Pen & Sword
MILITARY

First published in Great Britain in 2005 by
Pen & Sword Military
an imprint of
Pen & Sword Books Limited
47 Church Street
Barnsley
South Yorkshire
S70 2AS

ISBN 1-84415-251-0

A CIP catalogue record for this book is available from the British Library

Typeset in 10pt Palatino by Mac Style, Scarborough, N. Yorkshire

Printed and bound in the UK by
CPI UK Ltd

Pen & Sword Books incorporates the imprints of Pen & Sword Aviation, Pen & Sword Maritime, Pen & Sword Military, Wharncliffe Local History, Pen & Sword Select, Pen & Sword Military Classics and Leo Cooper.

For a complete list of Pen & Sword titles please contact:
PEN & SWORD BOOKS LIMITED
47 Church Street, Barnsley, South Yorkshire, S70 2AS, England
email: enquiries@pen-and-sword.co.uk
website: www.pen-and-sword.co.uk

Contents

Preface

Agincourt is one of England's most famous victories. The story has been told many times but I believe there is still much to say about it. My particular interest is in the psychology of battle – what motivated men to fight, even in the most difficult and desperate of circumstances. I put Henry V's inspirational generalship at the heart of my story and look at its effect on the morale of his army. I am grateful to Rupert Harding of Pen and Sword Books for his encouragement and feedback as this project got under way, and to Alan Rooney of Midas Battlefield Tours, with whom I have worked for many years, for giving me the chance to take people around the Agincourt battle site.

A number of people have offered me sterling support. Dr Rowena Archer shared with me her ideas on the battle – particularly on the archers' protective stakes – and generously allowed me to draw upon the household account of John Mowbray, earl of Norfolk – the marshal of Henry V's army – set out in her Oxford DPhil thesis. Dr Matthew Strickland read through my work and made many valuable comments and kindly wrote the foreword. I have benefited considerably from Matthew's recent book, co-written with Robert Hardy, *The Great Warbow*, which is destined to become a 'soldiers' bible' for the late Middle Ages. Professor Clifford Rogers made a huge contribution, reading and commenting on my text as it progressed and making available his important research on the Agincourt campaign. Professor Christopher Allmand encouraged the book forward, saving me from a number of errors and sharing his ideas on Vegetius, the Roman military writer who profoundly influenced medieval battle strategy. Last but not least, Dr David Grummitt checked through the completed work and advised me on a number of points. To all I am enormously grateful.

I have talked to the students of Durham University history society about my ideas on the battle and greatly benefited from a discussion with Professor Michael Prestwich on medieval military leadership and a comparison between the two great warrior kings, Henry V and Edward I. It has also been a privilege to speak to the East Anglian branch of the Battlefields Trust at Erpingham House, within walking distance of the church where that most distinguished Agincourt veteran, Sir Thomas Erpingham, constructed the great tower – spelling out his name and achievement for posterity.

Geoffrey Wheeler's picture research has enriched this book and I have benefited from his insights into the making of the Olivier film, *Henry V*. Others who have given particular assistance are acknowledged in the endnotes. I hope readers will be encouraged to visit the site of Agincourt – the chapter on the battlefield today develops my different rendition of this famous clash of arms. I have been greatly helped in all this by the support and feedback of my wife Liz. This book is especially dedicated to my younger son Rufus, whose fight for life inspired me.

A Note on the Sources

Keith Dockray's *Henry V* (Tempus, 2004) gives an excellent introduction to the full range of chronicle sources for the king's reign; Malcolm Mercer's *Henry V: The Rebirth of Chivalry* (National Archives, 2004) provides a useful sample of some of the documentary material. All the accounts of Agincourt have been gathered in Anne Curry's *The Battle of Agincourt: Sources and Interpretations* (Boydell & Brewer, 2000) – abbreviated in the endnotes as 'Curry, *Sources*' – and this is the indispensable companion for any study of the battle.

Using chronicle sources for Agincourt can be a frustrating exercise. Their accounts can be contradictory and it is sometimes difficult to make sense of them. Yet they remain our best guide to such an extraordinary event. Documentary material, however valuable, rarely catches the powerful emotions which drove men to fight – or allows us to glimpse the morale of the soldiers readying themselves for battle. And it is the chroniclers who open a window for us onto the all-important effects of leadership and motivation in combat.

One source stands out amongst the rest – the testimony of a chaplain who accompanied Henry's expedition, known as the *Gesta Henrici Quinti* (The Deeds of Henry V). This superb eye-witness – referred to as the chaplain's account in the text – gets to the heart of events and gives a real sense of the mood of the English army.

I have also given a particular emphasis to Titus Livius's *Vita Henrici Quinti* (Life of Henry V) because it draws substantially on the recollections of the king's brother, Humphrey duke of Gloucester. It is undeniably partisan but nevertheless carries real immediacy and authenticity.

I am grateful to Keith Dockray who has kindly discussed with me the best way to use some of this material.

Timeline – Henry V and the Agincourt Campaign

1386	Henry born at Monmouth Castle
1399	Deposition of Richard II; Henry's father takes the throne as Henry IV
1400	Revolt of Owen Glendower breaks out in Wales
1403	Henry IV defeats Hotspur at the battle of Shrewsbury
1409	Collapse of Glendower's rebellion
1413	Death of Henry IV; his son – Henry V - succeeds him
1415	Henry V invades France (13 Aug.)
	Henry captures Harfleur (22 Sept.)
	Henry defeats the French at the battle of Agincourt (25 Oct.)
1416	French fleet defeated by the English in the Seine
1417–19	Henry V conquers Normandy
1420	Treaty of Troyes – marriage of Henry and Katherine of Valois
1421	Henry V's brother, the duke of Clarence, defeated and killed at Baugé
1422	Death of Henry V

Foreword

The battle of Agincourt, fought on 25 October 1415, was viewed by contemporaries as an awesome and cataclysmic event. To the English, the triumph of King Henry V and his men over a mighty French army was not only a return to the glory days of Edward III and the Black Prince, but also seemed nothing less than the judgement of God, made manifest in a trial by battle, on the righteousness of the king's claim to France. To the French, the battle was an unmitigated calamity, 'this piteous and saddest of days', in which many of their greatest nobles perished and the proud chivalry of France suffered a humiliating defeat at the hands of mere archers. Not since Crécy in 1346 had there been such a military catastrophe for French arms, and the country was plunged into political upheaval and intense soul searching. The sense of shock, bewilderment, shame and tragedy still movingly reverberates through the outpouring of writings that followed the battle. How was it that such a powerful army, led by princes of blood, which had intercepted Henry's army on its weary march to the safety of Calais and which had drawn up with such confidence that fateful morning between the woods of Tramecourt and Agincourt, was then so utterly vanquished by a smaller force, tired, bedraggled and ridden with dysentery?

It is a question which has continued to intrigue historians ever since, and the one which lies at the heart of this book. All too often, concentration on a detailed campaign narrative, with the focus on logistics, strategy and tactics, has led historians either to ignore or to marginalize the crucial dimension of the actual experience of war itself – of what motivated men to fight, and of how commanders sought to 'thaw cold fear' and to inspire courage and resolve during the hardships of campaign and above all in the face of the enemy. Here, by contrast, Michael Jones offers a fresh new interpretation of the events of 1415 by focusing on the psychological dimensions of medieval military leadership and of combat. How was it that Henry V roused his men to press home the hard-fought but ultimately successful siege of Harfleur, when many had been killed and still more invalided home by the terrible 'bloody flux' that swept the army? How too did he inspire his men to fight and win on St Crispin's Day, when want of provisions, sickness and fear of the enemy's strength might well have sapped their courage? And how on the battlefield itself did the English turn a potential catastrophe into a resounding victory?

The answer, Jones argues, lies not simply in the quality of the English men-at-arms and archers, equipped with the formidable longbow, but in Henry's genius as a commander. Through a number of masterfully employed vignettes, we are shown Henry's natural ability to strike a chord with his soldiers, deftly treading the fine line between 'the common touch' and the need to inspire the awe, respect and even fear that was vital to the successful practice of kingship. But if Henry was 'the archers' general', he knew too how to win the fierce loyalty not only of his great lords but of the gentry who formed the bulk of his men-at-arms. As the author shows, men did indeed 'remember with advantages' many years later how the king had rewarded them for their acts of courage and good service - men such as Sir John Fastolf, granted lands where Henry's army landed in 1415 for being the first to reach French soil, or Thomas Strickland, a hard-up Westmorland squire nonetheless honoured by the king who made him the royal standard bearer on the campaign for his past bravery. We see too his calculated use of ritual, such as the invocation of saints and the wearing of the royal regalia, to bury the potentially disastrous dissensions of his father's reign in a common cause against the old enemy, France, and to strengthen his soldiers' resolve before battle.

In emphasizing the importance of battlefield psychology in medieval warfare, Michael Jones is writing in the tradition of such authors as the great Belgian military historian J F Verbruggen, whose pioneering study, *The Art of Warfare in Western Europe during the Middle Ages* (1954), attempts to discover the mind-set of men in combat, and Sir John Keegan, whose equally groundbreaking work *The Face of Battle* (1976) offers a remarkable attempt to reconstruct the soldier's experience of battle through a comparative study of Agincourt, Waterloo and the Somme. Yet for the fifteenth century, it is an approach which Jones has made very much his own. He has already used his understanding of chivalric culture with great effect to bring to light the remarkable English victory at Avranches in 1439, and to offer major reinterpretations of the battle of Verneuil in 1424, called 'a second Agincourt', and, most recently, of the battle of Bosworth in 1485. His present study of Agincourt itself displays the same ability to bring to his analysis an understanding of the wider cultural, religious and political context, to listen with empathy to the sources as contemporary voices, and above all to put himself in the minds of medieval commanders and their soldiers. This is 'chivalric military history', not in the sense that it concentrates on an aristocratic elite – for Jones is at pains to see the campaign as much through the eyes of Henry's archers as through those of the king himself – but because it highlights the gestures, ritual, and motives that a fifteenth-century army would have instinctively acknowledged and which played such a central role in their experience of battle.

Not that the importance of strategy, tactics or the actual business of fighting is forgotten. Here Michael Jones argues that, contrary to many traditional interpretations of the 1415 campaign, Henry was not attempting to avoid a major battle with the French on his northern march from Harfleur to Calais but was in fact seeking a decisive engagement. This was because, as Professor Anne Curry has recently shown, the French only originally intended to muster an army of some 9,000 men, while Henry's own strength on leaving Harfleur was around 8,000. But whereas Curry goes on to suggest that the English were still not greatly outnumbered by the time of Agincourt itself, with the French army being perhaps no greater than 12,000 men, Jones argues forcefully that, by late October, Henry *did* face overwhelming odds, as many of the chronicle sources emphasize. A new found sense of unity and resolve in the face of external invasion, completely unexpected by Henry when he began his march, served massively to swell the ranks of the French army and confronted the English king with imminent disaster. How the king saved his army from this terrible crisis by exhortation, ruse and sheer hard fighting is suggested in the climax of this book. A bold reinterpretation of aspects of the battle itself will doubtless provoke fresh debate, but this vivid and compelling account captures the mood of a fight so desperate that, in a last resort, Henry was driven to order the killing of the noble French prisoners. When at last the combat abated, the king had to enquire of the heralds whether he had actually won the battle. Even the English were appalled at the terrible slaughter which had taken place, and stunned by so great a victory. Henry ordered his men to ascribe the triumph not to themselves but to God, for all realized that something extraordinary had taken place on that fateful October day. Here Michael Jones takes us into the ranks of the English army from the siege of Harfleur to the field of Agincourt, to discover how King Henry and his men achieved one of the most remarkable of medieval feats of arms.

Dr Matthew Strickland
University of Glasgow

CHAPTER I

Rediscovering Agincourt

On 25 October 1415 a small English army won a spectacular victory on the muddy fields of France. They were heavily outnumbered by their French opponents and terribly weakened by dysentery, yet they achieved an astonishing success. Scores of the enemy's chief aristocrats were killed or captured; thousands of their fellow countrymen were slain. It was a staggering result – and one that has had a huge impact on our history, folklore and legend.

I want to share this story with you – and try to get across its sheer power: the fear and uncertainty felt by the English troops on the march and the extraordinary heroism they displayed on the battlefield. I will follow in the footsteps of this remarkable army, revisiting the bloody siege of Harfleur, the dangerous campaign across northern France and its incredible culmination at Agincourt. I want to put you in the shoes of the English soldiers, give you a sense of what motivated them to fight and, hopefully, draw you closer to this long-vanished army and its remarkable commander.

Celebration of Agincourt's invigorating success started soon after the event. The battle's winner, Henry V, was a shrewd self-publicist and he put out a simple yet powerful idea – that of a boy David defeating a giant Goliath – in his stage-managed victory procession. As the king and his entourage reached London, the capital prepared a series of pageants so all could see this triumph of the underdog. This motif was quickly circulated in newsletters, chronicles and most remarkably in song. The Agincourt Carol set the English

Henry V's triumphant return to London after his victory at Agincourt struck a timeless chord: here is how the Victorians imagined it.

victory to rousing music and guaranteed as many people as possible got to hear of it.

The ballad was almost certainly composed around the time of the king's spectacular entry into the capital on 23 November 1415. The city was packed – as one of Henry's chaplains tells us, 'so great was the throng of people in Cheapside, from one end to the other, that the horsemen were only just able, although not without difficulty, to ride through'. A choir had gathered to perform 'a song of congratulation'. And the refrain would have been sung out lustily to musical accompaniment:

> Our king went forth to Normandy
> With grace and might of chivalry
> There God for him wrought marvellously
> Wherefore England may call and cry
> To God give thanks for the victory.

Nowadays we are used to such spin operations and regard them with cynicism. But here a significant point was being made. As

Henry rode into London a bevy of maidens greeted him with a musical fanfare, beating drums and strumming gilt viols. This was a deliberate imitation of a biblical scene of David returning from the slaughter of Goliath and this was quickly understood by the onlookers. As one contemporary, Adam of Usk, remarked, the whole city was en fête and the simple motif that followed struck everybody. As Henry V approached Cheapside:

> Chanting virgins came dancing to meet him, accompanied by choirs and drums and golden viols, just as in King David's time, after the slaying of Goliath. What more can I say? The city wore its brightest aspect, and happiness filled the people – and rightly so.

Adam of Usk was not some naive observer, swept along by a superficial tide of emotion. Later in the reign he actually became a critic of the war, saying bluntly: 'the lord king is now fleecing anyone with money, rich or poor, throughout the realm, in readiness

A mural by Adam Kokowski, dating from 1965, showing the Lord Mayor greeting Henry and his troops on their return. (North Peckham Civic Centre, London)

for his return to France'. This outburst makes his spontaneous patriotism in 1415 all the more telling. Adam was so moved by the triumph at Agincourt that he put a poem in his text, and translated from the Latin it reads:

> People of England, cease your work and pray
> For the glorious victory of Crispin's Day,
> Despite their scorn for Englishmen's renown,
> The odious might of France came crashing down.

Here it is – the 'odious might' of the French laid low by the humble few. Another piece of London street theatre, showing a tiny figure winning victory against a huge opponent, carried the same resonance. The chronicler Thomas Walsingham underlined the point: 'a triumph of a dwarf against a giant'. That was how everyone saw the battle.

We need to understand that the mood of celebration in the capital was heightened because of earlier pessimism that the outnumbered English army might have suffered a terrible defeat. Indeed, on the day of battle itself, a rumour was circulating in London that Henry and his men had been wiped out. Although no one knew precisely what was happening, this 'lamentable report, replete with sadness and cause for endless sorrow' suggests Henry's chances of survival were not rated highly. London's citizens feared the English army had suffered a catastrophe in France. Now it was all so different – despair had been transformed into a joyous triumph.

Not only had the underdog triumphed, he had done so with incredibly light casualties. The English dead were but a handful – at most scarcely more than a hundred; while the French had lost thousands. Many of these thousands had piled up in a macabre wall of bodies, as men collided with each other, slipped in the mud and were asphyxiated by the press of fighters behind them. Almost every noble family in France was afflicted with the loss of a father, brother, friend or kinsman.

Medieval society was struck by the image of fortune's wheel, and how at its zenith, when all seemed disposed for success, it was possible to plunge into disaster. The French had been so confident – on 25 October a premature report of their success had reached the nearby town of Abbeville, on the crossing point of the Somme, and a feast had been prepared to celebrate the imagined victory. The reality was too ghastly to contemplate. The University of Paris held a special service for the dead:

> The nation is inconsolable ... in battle against the English at Agincourt so many princes, nobles, knights and barons of the blood of France have been killed that there are few in the whole country who have not lost fathers, brothers or friends in the fighting.

However, the picture of the valiant few overcoming vastly superior opponents has now come under sustained attack. Anne Curry is a leading authority on the battle and has undertaken a thorough study of the chronicle and documentary evidence. In a recent book, *Agincourt: A New History*, she argues that the English were not substantially outnumbered at all. She estimates that Henry V's army was larger than we have thought, close to 9,000 in number, and the French far fewer, at most 12,000 strong. The picture of a small army defeating a much greater one is dismissed as clever propaganda. We are told that the story of the English fighting against desperate odds is just plain wrong. The implications of this argument are enormous. If correct, it would totally change the nature of the battle and the way we understand and celebrate it. And we would lose the power of one of Shakespeare's most famous speeches, Henry V's St Crispin's Day appeal to his troops, into the bargain. The book contains a host of new insights and valuable information. But I strongly challenge its overall interpretation. I believe the traditional view of the battle remains the right one.

We need to remember that David pitching in against mighty Goliath is not the invention of the London victory pageant; it is consistent with the way most contemporaries, both French and English, saw the battle. Henry V's chaplain recorded the terrified reaction of the English scout who first caught sight of the opposing French. Riding to the top of the ridge at Blangy, on the afternoon of 24 October, the day before the battle, he saw the enemy streaming across the valley beneath him, 'filling a very wide field, as with an innumerable host of locusts'. The frightened man galloped back to his master, the duke of York, one of Henry's chief aristocrats: 'with the utmost speed his horse would carry him ... and being almost breathless, said "Quickly, be prepared for battle, as you are just about to fight against a world of innumerable people"'.

Another English chronicler, Thomas Walsingham, stressed the opposing army was so vast its marching columns looked 'like so many forests, covering the country far and wide'. His vivid phrase conveys the likely eye-witness testimony of soldiers in Henry's army.

Medieval chronicles are notoriously vague about numbers and it does seem that many, on both sides, were unsure just how large the French army was. But we should be wary of a small minority of French sources which try to suggest that the two armies were of roughly the same size – the line of argument that Anne Curry is now putting forward. The majority of French accounts believed their forces outnumbered the English at a ratio of between 3 and 6 to 1. The chronicler Pierre Fenin put it simply: 'the French were incomparably greater in number than the English'.

I do think this was an astonishing English military triumph. The Agincourt Carol is rightly memorable, for setting Henry's victory celebration to music was an inspired idea. One of its contributors was likely to have been a foremost composer of the day, Lionel Power. Power served in the household of Henry's brother, Thomas, duke of Clarence, and was accomplished in a wide variety of musical styles. He was author of the first manuscript of titled English music – we might liken it to an early version of our modern chart toppers. Clarence encouraged him to compose a rousing *Sanctus* for the king's victorious return to London.

Clarence had his own issues with the war in France which were to bring him to a tragic end. He had missed out on Agincourt, being sent home with dysentery after the siege of Harfleur, and whatever his enthusiasm for musical celebration, his absence from that great victory still rankled. Six years later, in 1421, on campaign at Baugé but feeling little better, he endeavoured to win some renown of his own on the fields of France with an impromptu decision to charge into battle halfway through his evening meal. In his haste he left behind most of his archers. His experienced captains remonstrated with him, but he retorted that they had been at Agincourt and he had not. The man who loved putting battles to music sadly misjudged the tempo of the occasion: his small and hastily assembled army was overwhelmed and Clarence himself was quickly slain.

The discomfort he felt is understandable, for those who were present at Agincourt never forgot the experience. Alongside the status of the victorious soldiers, Clarence felt his inferiority keenly. After Edward I's successful invasion of Scotland in 1296, popular songs – some sung by the ordinary soldiers – spread information and enthusiasm about the war. In the wake of Agincourt a host of popular poems and ballads soon sprang up and the poet John Lydgate caught the general mood of amazement:

> ... When, without stratagem,
> But in plain shock and even play of battle,
> Was ever known so great and little loss
> On one part and on th'other? Take it, God,
> For it is none but thine!

Over the years the legend of this astonishing triumph grew and grew. Its most famous depiction is William Shakespeare's *Henry V*. The play immortalizes the deeds of the valiant army with a series of exemplary speeches: 'Once more unto the breach ...', 'we few, we happy few ...' Shakespeare's impact has been brought to our modern era through the cinema. It is no coincidence that Sir Laurence Olivier decided to film *Henry V* during the Second World War. As Olivier said, it 'was a play appropriate to the time, for it tells of unconquerable spirit ... the feeling of unity which draws all together in the hour of danger'. The resonance of a great English turnaround, a victory against all the odds, was wonderfully strong. Agincourt represented a miracle where only bitter defeat had seemed a possibility.

There are many themes of Englishness to be found here. The red cross of St George on its white background had become a remarkable symbol of unity for the beleaguered English army – the same insignia adopted with enthusiasm at our big sports fixtures today. Then there is a powerful English symbol of plucky defiance – the V sign. By the Victorian period there was a strong belief that it had originated from the battle. Its provenance is uncertain, although contemporary sources do tell us of a French threat to cut off the bowstring fingers of the English archers. The raising of these fingers, defiantly intact, could well have been a derisive salute against the enemy. According to one chronicler, Henry addressed his bowmen in the following fashion:

> He reminded them that the French had boasted that they would cut off three fingers from the right hand of every archer they might capture, in order that they might never presume again to shoot at man or horse.

The problem lies in the arithmetic. If the enemy had threatened to cut off the three bowstring fingers, it seems unlikely that the English archers would show two instead in a V-sign. Yet even if this satisfying explanation is incorrect, the underlying sentiment is right. The bowmen, who formed the vast majority of the English army, were mostly recruited from the ordinary peasantry, a class that the French had scarcely deigned to recruit from at all. Theirs was a largely aristocratic force and this class distinction gave a particular relish to their subsequent humiliation and defeat – and equally heightened the French sense of shame.

I do believe that humble David bringing down the giant Goliath is more than clever propaganda. I see it telling us something important about the battle. Ordinary English soldiers had triumphed against the French aristocratic elite – and this is why the military achievement of Agincourt is rightly a source of great pride. At the beginning of the fourteenth century, the chronicler Jean Le Bel derided the English army as the laughing stock of Europe. Within a generation our fighting force had shown its mettle in the campaigns of Edward III and achieved famous victories at Crécy and Poitiers with a particularly effective weapon – the longbow. Agincourt therefore represents the culmination of the longbow's success. The bow required years of training to use properly. The English kings of the twelfth and thirteenth centuries had relied heavily on Welsh archers to supply the majority of their bowmen, but by the late Middle Ages its use was widespread amongst English troops. Its speed and range made it a much-feared weapon. It was the highest compliment to our bowmen that by the early fifteenth century the Grand Master of the Teutonic Knights, the toughest chivalric order in Europe – with the same kudos as our modern SAS – began to recruit substantial numbers of English archers. The French dramatically underestimated their effect.

Alongside the longbow, we need to take account of an English army that performed with a remarkable discipline and professionalism and above all demonstrated its strong sense of unity at a moment of crisis. In this sense it is more than just a battle – it is a genuine coming-of-age for the nation, a rite of passage that lives with us as strongly as Blenheim or Waterloo.

I believe the best way to get to grips with this battle is to retrace the route of Henry V's army as it crossed France and ended up on those muddy fields on a cold, wet October morning in 1415. There

Arthur de Richemont – he conducted Agincourt's first ever battlefield tour in June 1436.

is much to be gained from such a journey, and many have undertaken it. Intriguingly, Agincourt boasts one of the earliest recorded battlefield tours. In the summer of 1436 one of the combatants, Arthur de Richemont, now constable of France, returned to the scene of the action with a small group of followers. Richemont had been left for dead under a huge mound of French corpses. He was later pulled out, unconscious, and put to ransom. It must have been a powerful moment for him as he deliberately returned to the battle site with his companions. His memory of the preliminaries was clear enough. He pointed out where the great

French lords had camped and, little more than half a mile away, the spot where the king of England had set up his great tent. But Richemont was reluctant to talk about the battle itself. He recalled the ferocity of the French assault on Henry V's position and how some of the king's kinsmen, standing close by him, were slain or wounded. But how the English managed to win so decisively, against the odds, was too painful for him to contemplate. Richemont summed it up with a brief and rueful comment, 'God was not with us that day'.

One wishes he had been able to say more. Yet Richemont did stress the importance of the terrain: 'the field of battle was too narrow' – the space was too confined for the numerically superior French, who were funnelled towards the English line. This proved disastrous as the battle unfolded. Revisiting the site of the battle will help us grasp the scale of the English achievement. But first we need to recall some of the most powerful depictions of the Agincourt story.

As I have mentioned, one of the battle's most memorable renditions is Sir Laurence Olivier's 1944 film *Henry V*. The genius of the film lies in its straightforward portrayal of military heroism. It was made shortly before the Allied landings on the Normandy beaches and dedicated to 'the Commandos and Airborne troops of Great Britain – the spirit of whose ancestors it has humbly been attempted to recapture in some ensuing scenes'. Olivier's film caught the energy of real leadership from the front – and the scenes of Henry addressing his men before the breach at Harfleur are genuinely inspiring. So too is its inclusive vision of English patriotism – with careful attention given to the English bowmen and their preparations to withstand the French attack.

Olivier filmed *Henry V* in Ireland, at Enniskerry, 30 miles south of Dublin. Sir Laurence's leadership from the front took on a quite literal meaning as some of the self-proclaimed 'Irish stuntmen' (in fact local farmers, looking for a little extra cash), who endearingly addressed him as 'Mr Oliver', showed a worrying reluctance to display their skills. Finding one bowman constantly boasting of his ability but never demonstrating it, an increasingly exasperated 'Mr Oliver' challenged him to hit a named target. The arrow misfired so drastically it struck the director in the leg. Fortunately Henry V's bowmen were made of sterner stuff. Regular practice and considerable skill were necessary in order to become an effective archer. The sheer arrogance of the French aristocracy led them to denigrate the English bowmen – and they paid for it in terrible fashion.

The Italian producer Filippo del Giudice had encouraged the film venture – wanting to recreate a classic English triumph in time of war – and Olivier responded in stirring fashion, giving Henry both majesty and natural heroism. This king, the actor and director said, 'always managed to be inspiring at the right moment'. Winston Churchill supported the project, thinking *Henry V* ideal for the country at the time of the D-Day landings. The king's victory against the odds had already provided inspiration when Churchill paid tribute to our airforce pilots during the Battle of Britain, famously drawing upon the image of Henry V's 'happy few': 'Never in the field of conflict was so much owed by so many to so few'. The version Olivier produced is unashamedly heroic and patriotic yet it catches a real and fundamental truth about Agincourt.

But in keeping the message simple and clear, Olivier inevitably oversimplifies and omits some of the dilemmas facing Henry and his army. We do not see how Henry was forced to confront a conspiracy of rebellious nobles before he sailed from Southampton, or how he needed to make the threat to storm Harfleur and put it to the sword to induce its final capitulation. And the king's controversial order, twice repeated in Shakespeare's *Henry V*, that the French prisoners at Agincourt be put to death – leading to a cold-blooded massacre, one of the most terrible decisions Henry was ever forced to make – is also left out.

This selective editing of the story is seen most strongly in the surrender negotiations at Harfleur. Henry V threatened the town with an all-out assault unless his terms were accepted, and Shakespeare caught the violence of the English king's threat. In the play, the king warns Harfleur's commander of what might follow:

> The gates of mercy shall all be shut up
> And the fleshed soldier, rough and hard of heart
> In liberty of bloody hand shall range …

Henry creates a ghastly picture of the sack of the town by his unrestrained soldiery – one of rape, murder and pillage – and then issues a stark warning:

Therefore you men of Harfleur,
Take pity of your town and of your people,
While yet my soldiers are in my command.

This had a frightening historical echo. On Edward III's Crécy campaign in 1346 the king was held back at the town of Caen – and after his troops finally broke down the defences they went on a rampage of killing, raping and plundering. The incident became notorious, for as the chronicler Froissart related, Edward made little effort to restrain his men, declaring that the town had 'cost him all too dear' and would have to be punished to discourage others from resistance. Sometimes a medieval commander had to be utterly ruthless. But the infliction of such horrors upon civilians is rightly disturbing to us. This was not something either Churchill or Olivier wished to dwell on when the film came out in 1944.

The picture of the battle was also simplified. In the Olivier film, a line of French horsemen assembles, representing the glittering might of chivalry. It is opposed by mud-splattered, honest English archers. The imposing cavalry line moves forward, only to be met by a hail of arrows. Horse after horse plunges to the ground. This main theme of the battle scene is modified by modern scholarship. In reality the cavalry attack was actually much more modest – a small number of horsemen, attacking from the wings. The main French advance was on foot – slower, although still dramatic. Yet the scenes of preparation for battle, with the bowmen hammering in their protective stakes and the French knights toasting the likelihood of easy victory, still ring true. The finery of knights and nobles is well portrayed – and such lavish display was a vital part of medieval chivalry. In its own way, the film still gives us the best introduction to the spirit of the battle.

However, the happy certainty of the Olivier film was in historical reality only reached after terrible hardship. For a chaplain who accompanied Henry V's army, and subsequently gave us one of the best accounts of campaign and battle, it was a story of a miraculous recovery where defeat had seemed almost inevitable. In the chaplain's version, the battle of Agincourt was a desperate stand after a series of disasters. The English army had first run into difficulties at Harfleur, where they lost many men to dysentery, with more being sent home. Henry V then took a risky decision – to march his reduced force to English-held Calais. Things went rapidly wrong. The crossing point of the River Somme was held by the enemy and the English were forced further and further up-river. They eventually hazarded a crossing but by now a large French army was gathering to block their route to Calais. The starving English became increasingly demoralized. In French accounts – although there is no mention of this in English sources – Henry was so desperate that he opened negotiations with the enemy, offering to surrender all that he had won on campaign and pay a large ransom, in return for a safe passage home. His opponents, sensing an easy victory, refused. And yet, out of this calamitous situation, Henry somehow managed to inspire his men to hold firm on the narrow, muddy field of battle. The French totally underestimated the new-found resolve of the English army and were quite miraculously defeated.

War was a tough trade and one experienced soldier of the late Middle Ages – Geoffrey de Charny – warned prospective warriors of its harsh realities: 'You will have to put up with great labour before you achieve honour from this employ: heat, cold, fasting, hard work, little sleep and long watches and exhaustion'. Charny emphasized that battle was terrifying and the sight of soldiers in bloody combat made many want to flee rather than stay and fight. It is this mood of grim realism which is brought out in Kenneth Branagh's 1989 *Henry V*– a very different depiction of the battle. The awfulness of the conditions is rightly stressed: the terrible clinging mud, the crush of soldiers that made movement so difficult. We are shown an ugly slaughter-house – a killing field. By focusing on the brutal realities of the conflict, we are able to see the workings of luck, barely grasped opportunity and, above all, random chance.

Both film accounts tell important truths. But I want to give a different emphasis to my own story of the Agincourt campaign and battle. I want to look at the qualities of leadership Henry V displayed, show what made his army tick and how it held together on the vital march. I will stress the medieval understanding of morale and motivation at times of war and look for underlying factors that contributed to an English victory.

The French had assembled a mighty force to oppose the English, but for the medieval military theorist size was not everything. Battle commentators recognized dangers in deploying an over-large army. Just a few years before Agincourt, the French writer Christine de Pisan brought out a military manual, *The Deeds of Arms and Chivalry*.

She argued against the view that victory would belong to the side with the most men. On the contrary, she emphasized that once an army became large and unwieldy it was far more difficult to maintain its cohesion and good order:

> Therein lies the difficulty, for the large army cannot move forward, but so many men will rather get in the way of each other, and in battle formation they lunge forward so hastily that they mingle needlessly with the enemy, and are exterminated.

Here Christine de Pisan was recalling a Roman military maxim: 'A greater multitude is subject to more mishaps'. Her warning that, if an advancing army was too big, its men would simply get in the way of each other, was remarkably prescient. But it was Henry V, not her intended French audience, who took heed of her message. The qualities praised by Christine, organization and intelligence in military operations, rather formed the bedrock of Henry's martial skill.

If an army was small, its chances of success depended on its discipline and morale. This is well brought out in a vignette famously enshrined in Shakespeare's play. On the morning of battle, amidst a gathering of wet, dispirited Englishmen, 'cousin Westmorland' bemoaned the number of the enemy. His unwelcome pessimism provided an awkward moment, for many of Henry's followers must have been thinking the same thing. What was the king to do? If he ignored Westmorland's doubts, he would show himself hopelessly out of touch with reality. If he confirmed them, he would admit the apparent hopelessness of the English position. Instead, in an inspired and inspiring rejoinder, Henry turned the situation around with one of the most famous speeches of the play:

> … No my fair cousin
> If we are marked to die, we are enough
> To do our country loss; and if to live,
> The fewer men, the greater share of honour.
> God's will, I pray thee wish not one man more.

And he powerfully built on this idea:

We few, we happy few, we band of brothers.
For he today that sheds his blood with me
Shall be my brother; be he ne'er so vile,
This day shall gentle his condition.

A great leader must win over the doubters: the stained-glass figures from the Royal Shakespeare Theatre, Stratford upon Avon, depict King Henry V (left) and the earl of Westmorland (right).

And gentlemen in England now abed
Shall think themselves accursed they were not here,
And hold their manhoods cheap whiles any speaks
That fought with us upon Saint Crispin's day.

No longer are the English hapless underdogs – they are a select band of brothers, chosen by God to take on the might of the French. It is a remarkable moment. To gain a sense of Shakespeare's skill, it is instructive to compare this speech with that in an earlier play, *The Famous Victories of Henry V*, which was probably first staged in 1588, a decade earlier than Shakespeare's own. In it, there is a striking anticipation of the scene where Henry rallies his troops but here the language lacks power and conviction:

My Lords and loving Countrymen,
Though we be few and they be many,
Fear not, your general is good, and God will defend you:
Pluck up your hearts, for this day we shall either have
A valiant victory, or an honourable death.

It is Shakespeare who instinctively catches the mood of the English army, for once again, this is a moment when the playwright is true to his sources. The eye-witness account of Henry's chaplain reveals such an incident really did happen, although it was on the day before battle, after the French host had first been sighted. In this contemporary account it is the aristocrat Sir Walter Hungerford who, in a moment of panic, wished for thousands more archers. The king publicly rebuked him, saying that those who were with him were specially chosen:

Though speakest foolishly, for by the God of Heaven, on whose grace I have relied, and in whom I have a firm hope of victory, I would not, even if I could, increase my number by one. For those whom I have are the people of God, whom He thinks are worthy to have at this time. Dost thou not believe that the Almighty, with these His humble few, is able to conquer the haughty opposition of the French.

He reminded Hungerford of the example of Judas Maccabeus, who had been promised God's support in battle but complained about

The garter stallplate of Sir Walter Hungerford at St George's Chapel, Windsor. In historical reality, it was Hungerford who wished that the English had more men.

his small numbers nonetheless. Surely, Maccabeus asked God, it would be better to wait for more troops? God told him to get on with it. Maccabeus did, and won.

Anne Curry is sceptical that this incident took place as described. However, I find the passage's detail plausible and convincing. It is supported by another account, that of Titus Livius, who drew on information supplied by the king's brother, Humphrey duke of Gloucester. Titus Livius puts the incident on the morning of battle with one of the king's captains – not named – overheard complaining: 'If only good God would grant that all those knights who are in England might be with us in this battle'. Henry's reply carries the same force and immediacy:

> I do not wish a single man to be added to my army. We are small in number ... May God and the justice of our cause defend us. May he render up all the multitude of that exceedingly proud enemy which you can see.

It is difficult for modern people to appreciate the effect this might have had in medieval times. As men's morale faltered before battle, a reference to what for us may be an obscure Old Testament character would be for them relevant and stirring. Judas Maccabeus was one of the nine worthies – one of the pantheon of warriors admired by late medieval society – and thus instantly recognizable to even the most stupid aristocrat. The chaplain's account is one of our best sources for the battle and I believe his recollection is authentic and important for the king's own father had likened himself to another Maccabeus. Henry regarded the story as a reminder of proper spiritual preparation before battle. The Dominican friar John Bromyard had written in the 1390s how God's help could be sought before combat, adding: 'Judas Maccabeus fasted and prayed before battle and thus he overcame his enemies'. This is a source I shall return to, for I believe Henry knew of Bromyard's writings and they strongly shaped his martial outlook. The broader context is important. When the chaplain shares with us the growing pessimism of the English army – increasingly fearful of the size of the enemy they will have to face – this is not stock propaganda. In his excellent new study of the English medieval soldier, Anthony Goodman emphasizes that this testimony 'carries particular conviction' because it portrays both the magnificence of the English victory and the army's previous dire straits. The chaplain tells us that, after their crossing of the Somme, English soldiers were terrified of the number of men ranged against them. Let us take one dramatic example. After the French had crossed the road from Péronne, the English, coming up behind, found it trodden 'by so many thousands' that they could only dread the impending battle. Here we have a window on the faltering morale of the army, chaplains and soldiers alike, all 'crying with voices of the deepest earnestness, for God to have compassion upon us, and, of his infinite goodness, to turn away from us the power of the French'. This grim backdrop makes an outburst of fear before the battle of Agincourt all too believable. And for the English army to be effective in battle, Henry would have to address these doubts head on. As I will emphasize in the following chapter, his inspirational reply was entirely characteristic of him.

This important episode reveals an underlying truth – in the midst of adversity Henry was able to make his army feel special. To turn such situations around is the sign of a truly gifted commander. We can look to another great English medieval warrior, King Edward I. Before the battle of Falkirk, in 1298, Edward's Welsh infantry ran off. The army was short of supplies and men feared the deserters might now join with their opponents. But Edward was unconcerned whether they joined the Scottish army. He exclaimed confidently: 'Both are my enemies and both will be defeated.' The king's resolve steadied his men's nerves.

Where did Henry pluck his own inspiration from? His chaplain gives us a spiritual explanation. He tells us that, at a time of dark despair, the night before the battle, Henry managed to find hope in the midst of his despondency. Out of his vigil and time alone with God came a renewed sense of purpose and devotion to a higher cause. This tells us part of the story. Henry was a man of deep religious faith who genuinely saw himself as God's chosen instrument. But we also need to credit him with the skill to motivate others. The human factor is so important – and I want to recreate the soldier's view.

How might this work? We know that on the march across France, when the English army was deliberately travelling light, Henry nevertheless chose to carry precious items of his royal regalia – including a crown and sword of state. Some of these were displayed outside Harfleur, when the king sat enthroned in majesty to receive the surrender of the town. Then they seem to have been intended for a ritual procession before the battle, for we know that Henry subsequently donned a magnificent battle crown, a circlet of gold embedded with precious jewels, welded to his helmet.

There are a number of meanings here and I want to explore them with you over the course of this book. The simplest shows Henry sharing the magnificence of kingship with his men and reminding them of his claim to the crown of France. He was also displaying exceptional courage. The king who took up position in the centre of his battle line was making himself a conspicuous target. This was a particularly brave act in light of experience at the battle of Shrewsbury in 1403 – where decoys dressed in Henry IV's coat of arms were killed in the fierce fighting around the royal standard. This risky but defiant gesture showed Henry willing to undergo the same risks as his soldiers. They were all in this together.

My own belief is that Henry created a real sense of unity within in his army from the outset. Agincourt was proof of his success. To understand the scale of his achievement, we need to look at the class-bound system of recruitment that late medieval warfare depended upon. The men-at-arms in Henry's army came primarily from the knightly class. These men had landed status, displayed a coat of arms and could afford horses and armour. John Mowbray, earl of Norfolk, was the marshal of Henry's army. In 1415 he commissioned an expensive new suit of steel plate armour for the expedition. It must have made an imposing sight. His equipment was not only up-to-date – its high-quality items procured from German armourers – but beautifully decorated with silver and gilt ornaments. The silk trappings alone, embroidered in gold thread, cost £40, more than four times the annual wage of an archer.

In contrast, most of the archers came from the ranks of the peasantry. They were skilled in using the bow through regular practice but only a few could afford expensive equipment to accompany it. The majority would count themselves lucky with a makeshift helmet and light chain mail shoulder coverings, and just a leather jerkin or jacket beneath. As a medieval army assembled to go to war, the class system was all too clearly represented in its weaponry and armour – or the lack of it. The French chronicler Pierre Cochon described the arrival of Henry V's archers at Harfleur with barely concealed disdain:

'Now thrive the armourers, and silken dalliance in the wardrobe lies' from Shakespeare's chorus. In fact it was the French who dressed up as if they were going to a tournament.

All with bare feet and no shoes, dressed in scruffy doublets made out of old bedding, a poor skull cap of iron on their heads, a bow and quiver of arrows in their hand and a sword hanging at their side. *That was all the armour that they had.* (My emphasis.)

And the Burgundian Monstrelet emphasized how at Agincourt most of the English archers 'were without armour, dressed in their doublets, their hose [trousers] loose around their knees, hanging axes or swords from their belts. Many had bare heads and were without headgear.'

The French seemed genuinely shocked that such poorly dressed men had the presumption to go into battle at all. In contrast, Jean de Waurin – who was present with the opposing army at Agincourt – described its participants turning up in all their finery, as if they were going to a tournament. The French were adhering to a strict dress code, arranging their ranks 'by invitation only' and pushing their squires and servants to the rear. But the English archers – seen by their opponents as 'scum', 'unworthy and vile' – would turn the battle through their skill and courage.

Pride in armour, seen in the late Middle Ages in tombs and memorial brasses, was thus a socially divisive marker, reminding us of the horrible dangers for those lower down the scale, with the least protection. In the terrible shock of impact, as one army clashed with another in the mêlée, the hand-to-hand combat between dismounted soldiers, the most lightly armoured were by far the most vulnerable. At this critical stage of fighting, aristocrats often showed scant interest in the fate of ordinary peasant soldiers and the instinctive reaction of these unfortunates was often just to get out of the way and run from the field. But Henry V had a very different vision for the Agincourt campaign, one which bridged the divide of class and equipment and forged a greater whole.

How might a medieval commander bring his army together? In the tense moments before battle there was little point in making a long-winded speech, which would not be heard by the majority of the troops anyway. Nor was it the moment for learned arguments giving a justification of the war with France. A medieval commander needed to put his case across simply and clearly, riding along the line, repeating the message to clusters of men, backed up by some sort of visual display – rather like our modern-day promotional company video – so that the ideas could quickly be digested and understood. With an army largely recruited from peasant stock and thus mostly illiterate, the effectiveness of such symbols would be all-important.

This is a very different language – where powerful sentiments are elaborated by ritual and gesture – and it is vital that we understand their meaning. I want to begin with one famous example, already introduced to you – the celebration of St Crispin's Day as a way of remembering the battle and the deeds of the English soldiers who fought there. It is captured memorably by Shakespeare:

> This day is called the Feast of Crispian.
> He that outlives this day and comes safe home
> Will stand a-tiptoe when this day is named
> And rouse him at the name of Crispian.
> He that shall see this day and live old age
> Will yearly on the vigil feast his neighbours
> And say, 'Tomorrow is Saint Crispian'.
> Then he will strip his sleeve and show his scars
> And say, 'These wounds I had on Crispin's day'.
> Old men forget; yet all shall be forgot,
> But he'll remember, with advantages,
> What feats he did that day. Then shall our names,
> Familiar in his mouth as household words …
> Be in their flowing cups freshly remembered.

And then, the theme is powerfully reiterated:

> This story shall the good man teach his son,
> And Crispin Crispian shall ne'er go by
> From this day to the ending of the world
> But we in it shall be remembered.

As we have seen, this powerful oration is based on solid historical fact, and such was Henry's veneration for these saints (the two, Crispin and Crispinian, were commemorated together) that he ordained that they should be celebrated in his daily masses in his own chapel for as long as he lived. He also ensured that their day, 25 October, would be properly observed in England on each returning anniversary of the battle. As one contemporary emphasized:

because that day was the commemoration by the church of the blessed Crispin and Crispinian, and it seemed to him it was through their intercession to God that he had obtained so great a victory over the enemy, he ordered that for as long as he lived commemoration of them was to be made in the masses which he heard every single day.

The explanation for this seems simple enough. The medieval calendar was based on its many saints days, and these were carefully set out in the beautifully illuminated books of hours that record the days and months, and whose scenes present to us an enduring image of medieval life. Their simple yet beautiful colour and design was an important influence on the sets produced for Olivier's *Henry V*. Since Agincourt fell on the saints day of Crispin and Crispinian it was therefore an obvious way of remembering it, particularly since Henry wanted credit for the victory to be given to God.

The capture and martyrdom of Sts Crispin and Crispinian – from a fifteenth-century painting at St Omer. Henry made this story powerfully relevant to his army: reminding them of the fate of their compatriots, slain in cold blood at Soissons in 1414.

*Memorial to Jean count of Roucy, one of the French aristocrats who died in the battle –
giving his date of death as 'the day of Sts Crispin and Crispinian'.*

But it is a surprising choice nonetheless, for Crispin and Crispinian were French saints, cobblers from Soissons who were martyred for their Christian beliefs late in the third century. Their story was well-known in France – it was depicted in a fine early fifteenth-century painting at Saint-Omer, not far from the Agincourt battle site – but would have unfamiliar to a wider English audience. In short, it was a French way of remembering the battle. This is brought out in a tomb engraving of one of the French slain, Jean count of Roucy: the memorial gives his day of death as 'the day of Sts Crispin and Crispinian'. Henry had fashioned an unusual honouring of an intrinsically English victory, one that caused Christopher Allmand, in his biography of the king, to draw attention to a seemingly 'audacious and ironic annexation of two French saints'.

Another saint's day fell on 25 October, and it was as unremarked upon as Crispin and Crispinian were celebrated: the feast of the translation of St John of Beverley. Yet it would seem a far more appropriate choice to remember Agincourt by. St John of Beverley was an English saint, whose piety was extolled by Bede and who had been canonized in the eleventh century. And in a clear martial precedent, his banner was used by Edward I, alongside that of St George, to encourage his soldiers on campaign. Importantly, St John of Beverley was closely connected with England's ruling dynasty. When Henry's father, Henry IV, had landed at Ravenspur in 1399, in his bid to take the throne, it was believed that the saint had shown approval of his actions: witnesses at his shrine claimed his body had distilled drops of oil at the time of Henry's return from exile. As a result, St John of Beverley was venerated by Henry V's family circle, and prayers to him are found in a number of their books of hours. This is an impressive pedigree. Remarkably, the saint was also said to have given a premonition of victory at Agincourt, again sweating out clear drops of oil at the very time that battle was ranging in Picardy.

Yet while St John of Beverley was acknowledged in the aftermath of Agincourt, it was Sts Crispin and Crispinian to whom 'the English people owed so much' – as the archbishop of Canterbury put it – who were singled out for special veneration. To favour French saints against such a notable English one was a quite extraordinary choice. And once we realize Henry was making a choice, we can look for the underlying meaning to make sense of his actions. I believe the key is that Crispin and Crispinian were martyrs of Soissons.

When Henry V invaded France the country was in the midst of bloody civil war. Two factions were competing for influence over its incapacitated king, Charles VI: one headed by the aristocratic house of Orléans (known as the Armagnacs), the other by the duke of Burgundy. The English had, from time to time, provided small-scale military assistance to one or other of the warring parties. In 1414 the Armagnacs regained Burgundian-held Soissons and subsequently put many of the garrison and ordinary townspeople to the sword. The incident became notorious and was well-known within Henry's army. When English soldiers entered the town of Harfleur they reassured its inhabitants: 'Fear not that we shall do you any harm! We shall not behave towards you as did your countrymen towards the people of Soissons, for we are good Christians.'

Crucially, amidst the garrison of Soissons had been a contingent of English archers. They had been sent into the service of the duke of Burgundy and – as foreign auxiliaries – should have been protected under the law of arms, the medieval equivalent of the Geneva Convention. But according to the Burgundian chronicler Monstrelet, a well-informed and reliable source, they were massacred in cold blood. This terrible deed could only have reinforced the prejudices of the ordinary bowmen: that they were not treated as proper combatants and were seen by the aristocracy as easily expendable.

By invoking Crispin and Crispinian at Agincourt Henry therefore venerated the slain archers of Soissons and honoured them as martyrs to the English cause. It was an astonishing mark of respect to England's bowmen. The king was reminding his men – through the massacre at Soissons – that they could expect no mercy from their opponents and therefore should not consider surrender or flight. Instead, they were fighting to avenge their fallen comrades.

Here we see Henry's gift as a commander: gestures such as this brought the whole army together and gave it a sense of common cause. As we follow the Agincourt campaign we will uncover many more. I believe they will give us a deeper understanding of this extraordinary victory. For this is the litmus test: how Henry communicated to his men, bound them together and gave them their motivation and self-belief, even in the most difficult and dangerous of circumstances. Let us gather with this army in the area of Southampton at the beginning of its story. It is early August, the year 1415 ...

CHAPTER II

A King Goes to War

In the summer of 1415 a 28-year-old man was gathering together the largest army England had seen for a generation. As Henry V installed himself at Portchester Castle, around 12,000 men were converging on the area between Southampton and Portsmouth, followed by a host of supporting workers. It was a formidable sight – a mass of soldiers, gunners, administrators, even royal musicians. And it was an army gathered for a mission: to invade France and reopen the ancient rivalry between the two countries we now know as the Hundred Years War.

What King Henry was doing was a bold but risky enterprise. Bold because England was emerging from a period of feuding and civil war and needed a strong unifying focus to bring the country together. Risky because the vast majority of England's soldiers were badly out of military practice and if it all went wrong Henry could be pushed off the throne altogether.

The leader of this great military expedition was the son of a man who had usurped the throne of England. In 1399 Henry's father, Henry IV, had come to power by deposing the anointed king, Richard II, subsequently imprisoning and almost certainly murdering him. As a result of these terrible actions Henry IV faced civil war and rebellion through most of his reign. His son's wish was to heal these divisions and unify the nation by offering it a new sense of mission. War in France fulfilled this objective.

To medieval society war could be a great and ennobling experience. It offered those who participated in it profit, fame and status. But it could also lead to death, injury or impoverishment. The

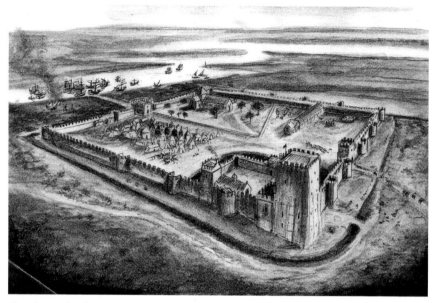

Portchester Castle – as it may have appeared when Henry V's army gathered at Southampton.

gain had to justify the risk. Reopening the war with France would have been seen by many of Henry's subjects as something of a mixed blessing. The fighting had ended badly in the late fourteenth century, with England on the receiving end of French naval attacks and war taxation increasingly unpopular. Whether it was a sense of personal destiny that prompted Henry to follow this path or merely political pragmatism, it required enormous courage. Henry had to make the course of action work. So let us take a closer look at the man himself.

This is not the place for an in-depth discussion of Henry V's kingship. But I do want to give you a sense of Henry as a war leader and commander of men – for without him, I do not think the English could have won at Agincourt. Observers of the time recognized his military gifts were outstanding – here are some of their verdicts.

The chaplain who accompanied the Agincourt expedition gave the following tribute to his leadership:

> our older men [do not] remember any prince ever having commanded his people on the march with more effort, bravery

or consideration, or having, with his own hand, performed greater feats of strength in the field.

Contemporaries were impressed by his courage: how Henry led from the front and thereby gave example to his men. Thomas Walsingham described how at Agincourt the king 'flung himself against the enemy. He both inflicted and received cruel blows, *offering an example in his own person to his men* by scattering the opposing lines with a battle axe' (my emphasis). A particular gift, picked up by one London chronicler of the time, was the king's ability to speak simply and directly to the ordinary soldier. The chronicler tells us that at the siege of Harfleur the king made a point of doing the rounds and encouraging his men. Henry's words seem to have been remembered verbatim and they are unaffected and entertainingly modern: 'Fellows be of good cheer! Save your energy, keep cool [be kele you well] and maintain your calm for, with the love of God, we shall have good tidings.' It is rather surprising to hear a fifteenth-century soldier exhorted to 'keep cool' five hundred years before the term entered general usage!

French chroniclers were struck by Henry's 'iron will', tough and forceful personality, rigorous military discipline and expertise in the latest technological thinking – at a time when such professionalism in war was rarely seen. The Monk of Saint-Denis remarked approvingly: 'No prince in his time appeared more capable to subdue and conquer a country'. Henry was a tough disciplinarian who set high standards for his men and expected them to be kept. But this French observer highlighted what I think was Henry's most outstanding skill, one extremely rare in an age where rank, status and social hierarchy counted for so much. We would call it effective man management: 'He made it a point of honour to treat everybody, of whatever rank or degree, with the utmost affability … he knew how to exalt the lowly'. Here it is in a nutshell – an observation which will guide us through the entire book. Henry was able to make the ordinary soldier feel special. So how did this come about? I will focus on some key examples, showing how such exceptional leadership ability was forged.

Medieval warfare recognized the value of an initiatory experience, where a man's martial qualities were welded together under the stress and danger of combat. An analogy can be made with the process of tempering a sword. To gain its full strength the weapon has to be subjected to intense heat. It is a time of great risk, for if the fire is too weak, the blade may subsequently crack during fighting, but if it is too strong, the blade will split in the flames themselves. Yet it is the vital moment. Through it is forged real durability in battle.

The great military historian of the medieval period, J F Verbruggen, understood this aspect well. He called it 'the whole psychology of the soldier'. The key to understanding a military campaign, he believed, lay in coming to grips with the state of mind of its participants, their desire for a fight or their fear of it:

> The essential element in each battle lies in the attitude of the soldiers during the fighting. The way they handle their weapons, the manner in which they react in the face of danger and behave in a battle for life – that is what counts.

The foremost war chronicler of the late Middle Ages – Jean Froissart – gives us a glimpse of what an initiatory experience might look like. Froissart vividly brought to life King Edward III's great fourteenth-century campaigns in France. His particular hero and model of leadership was Edward's son, the Black Prince. He wanted to give his readers a window onto his age and offer them an understanding of how great military leadership worked. He tells us that he set out his depiction of military events:

> In order that the honourable enterprises, noble adventures and deeds of arms which took place during the wars waged by France and England should be fittingly related and preserved for posterity, so that brave men should be inspired thereby to follow such examples.

Froissart picked out a crucial moment from an earlier great English victory, the battle of Crécy in 1346. King Edward III's army was under intense pressure from the repeated charges of the French cavalry. The division where his son, the Black Prince, was placed was bearing some of the hardest fighting. A worried messenger reached the king appealing for reinforcements. Edward replied bluntly: 'Let the boy win his spurs'.

This response might seem unnecessarily harsh, even shocking to us. Yet it is enormously instructive. There was obvious cause for anxiety – both about the fate of the king's son and the fear that the French might penetrate the English line. Yet Edward held firm. As he surveyed the emerging shape of the battle, the king saw it was clearly the wrong time to commit his reserve. But on a deeper psychological level, Edward also recognized that his soldiers needed to master their fear of the enemy's massed cavalry attacks. The business maxim warns us that we do not solve a problem by throwing money at it, and in the same way, the answer to a military crisis is not always to throw men at it. Edward's troops needed to face their terror of the charging horses of their opponents, hold together and find the resolve to win. I do not believe the king was foolhardy. He took the sensible precaution of sending a small, picked body of warriors to help maintain morale amongst the Black Prince's men. But he realized that this was a moment of truth for his army and his judgement was shown to be correct. The Black Prince stood his ground and the English army found the fresh

'Let the boy win his spurs': Edward III refuses to rush in to support his son at Crécy.

reserves of determination needed to bring about a memorable victory.

This was a powerful coming of age for the Black Prince. He went on to become an inspirational commander in his own right, winning great victories of his own at Poitiers and Najera. And he created an astonishing esprit de corps amongst the soldiers who followed him. Here Froissart understood an important truth. Only a commander who has undergone a meaningful initiation into the art of war can go on to initiate others and recreate the same spirit for his army.

This idea is important, for Henry V of England had faced an ordeal even more traumatic than that of the Black Prince at Crécy. Henry served his military apprenticeship not in France, but at a time of civil war within England and a bitter struggle against the rebellion of Owen Glendower in Wales. In 1403, at the age of 16, he fought in the battle of Shrewsbury against English rebels opposing his father. The clash revealed the fearsome power of the longbow – both sides employed a substantial number of archers and they inflicted considerable casualties. The storm of arrows unleashed by the rebels was so formidable that soon many were 'like apples fallen in the autumn, when stirred by the south-west wind', as the chronicler Thomas Walsingham vividly put it. Some of the royal army fled and a picked body of rebels, led by the young Henry Percy, son of the earl of Northumberland – nicknamed 'Hotspur' for his dash and courage – now launched an assault on Henry IV's main position. They hoped to quickly kill the king and gain a dramatic victory.

This was the crisis point of the battle. Several of those defending the king, including the royal standard bearer, were slain. The young Prince Henry had been seriously wounded by an arrow in the face, which lodged deep in the bone below the eye. But he refused to leave the field of battle, although the pain must have been agonizing, and instead launched his rearguard in support of his father's hard-pressed troops. Breaking through the mêlée, he struck against Hotspur's followers, a vital intervention which turned the battle around. Hotspur, rather than Henry IV, was slain in the fierce fighting that followed and the royal army won the day.

Contemporaries were impressed by Henry's presence of mind and particularly by his conspicuous bravery in the field. It was reported how, after he was wounded, he declared to the men around him that he would rather die than stain his reputation by flight. Titus Livius, who penned a life of Henry, caught his defiant address – and its tone seems authentic: 'Lead me, thus wounded, to the front line so that I may, as a prince should, kindle our fighting men with deeds not words.'

Henry's arrow wound left him in mortal danger for many weeks after the battle. His life was saved by the skill of a gifted surgeon – John Bradmore – who left a detailed account of the successful operation. When Bradmore was called to the prince he found he had been

> struck by an arrow next to his nose, on the left side, which entered at an angle, and after the arrow shaft was extracted, the head of the aforesaid arrow remained in the furthermost part of the bone of the skull for the depth of several inches.

Bradmore cut through the Prince's face to the depth of the wound, and then applied surgical tongs:

> I put these tongs in at an angle, in the same way as the arrow had first entered, then placed the screw in the centre and finally the tongs entered the socket of the arrowhead. Then, by moving it to and fro, little by little (with the help of God), I extracted the arrowhead. Many gentlemen and servants of the prince were standing by and all gave thanks to God.

The pain Henry endured, both from his horrible injury and the dramatic surgery which saved him, can hardly be imagined. Bradmore then spent days cleansing the wound and applying ointment to regenerate the flesh around it. He had saved the prince's life and the surgical procedure he devised was regarded as little short of miraculous.

After Bradmore's extraordinary efforts part of Henry's face would have been left heavily scarred. We are used to imagining him from the royal portrait now hanging in the National Portrait Gallery, which shows us the king's face unmarked. This picture was copied many years after the event, and presents an idealized version. But the ordinary soldier would have been immediately struck by Henry's battle scars. They told him everything he needed to know about his commander: that this was a man of outstanding courage, willing to take risks and lead from the front, exceptionally determined and, above all, favoured by God. As Anthony Goodman commented astutely, Henry's scarred face would have acted as a talisman for his troops.

The Black Prince gained his warrior's initiation at Crécy; Henry won his at Shrewsbury. Both went on to become notable leaders, winning famous battles and inspiring great loyalty from the soldiers following them. There can be no substitute for such formative experiences. For in a desperate situation, when morale is faltering and men are losing their nerve, the commander needs something real to fall back on, which he can then communicate to others, thereby uplifting their spirits. This cannot be faked. At the moment of crisis a military leader has to be absolutely authentic.

Shrewsbury gave Henry extraordinary self-belief. A glimpse of this inner conviction is seen shortly afterwards, in the fighting against the Welsh rebels of Owen Glendower. Early in 1405, after four years of hard effort to quell the revolt, it was reported with concern how these men were 'prouder and more confident than ever before'. The rebels had assembled a large army of 8,000 men and sacked the town of Grosmont. Prince Henry was only able to send a small army against them, numbering less than a thousand men, but his 'small power' routed the numerically superior enemy. Henry wrote to his father describing how the battle's outcome seemed to him like a 'miracle'. He then made a telling comment – one which strikingly foreshadowed the St Crispin's Day address before Agincourt: 'Yet it is known that victory is not in the multitude of the people, but in the power of God, and well was this shown.'

All the familiar ingredients are here: the small, heavily outnumbered army; the arrogance of an overconfident enemy and an abiding trust in the rightness of one's cause before God. When Henry's chaplain described the king making a similar appeal to his men before Agincourt, it was rooted in this strong sense of personal destiny.

Yet battle against fellow Englishmen at Shrewsbury or Glendower's rebels in Wales was a far cry from the glory of Crécy. Henry, like many aristocratic warriors, must have wondered where it had all gone wrong – why and how the great campaigns at the heyday of Edward III had degenerated into mismanaged fiascos by the 1380s. At the end of the fourteenth century the Dominican friar

John Bromyard wrote about war from a religious standpoint and offered his own explanation for England's military decline. Bromyard praised Edward III for going on pilgrimage before undertaking a war – and for taking the advice of those learned in God. He contrasted the king's spiritual preparation with the lax attitude of his successors:

> Yet nowadays, alas, princes and knights and soldiers go to war in a different spirit ... Recently a certain knight, noticing an English army going forth with such pride, commented that it looked more as if it were going to a wedding than going to war.

I believe Henry was familiar with Bromyard's work and strongly influenced by it. In 1408 the Oxford academic Richard Ullerston dedicated a book to him on the moral and spiritual requirements of being a knight, praising his 'desire for spiritual study' and commending him for his knowledge of the scriptures. Indeed from boyhood, Henry had acquired a reputation for serious reading – in English, French and Latin. Bromyard's message for the warrior was simple yet powerful: with the right preparation – and by seeking the help of God through prayer – anything was possible. Bromyard's writings emphasized one key idea, which Henry carried forward and embodied at Agincourt: 'For victory in battle is not achieved by the size of one's army, but by the help of God.'

What other lessons did Henry learn from Shrewsbury? After this bloody battle he fully understood the effectiveness of the English longbow and would have wished, on the Agincourt campaign, to weld these bowmen into a formidable fighting force, united under his command. His army would therefore be mostly composed of archers. Professor Curry has argued that the main reason Henry recruited so many archers was financial: they were paid at a lower daily rate and the king was short of money – it was all a mere cost-cutting exercise. I favour a more positive explanation: I believe he recruited so many because he wanted to defeat the French in battle.

The possibility of the humble archer winning battles went against the grain of the class-based society of the late Middle Ages. It saw warfare as an aristocratic pursuit and chivalry, the code of conduct which governed it, as the preserve of the nobleman. In short, medieval war was something of an exclusive, members-only club and riff-raff were most unwelcome. This was certainly the French viewpoint. The fifteenth-century French historian Juvenal des Ursins emphasized that Henry's soldiers were painfully aware of the cold-blooded murder of their compatriots at Soissons. The hapless archers captured there were treated as if the normal rules of war – scrupulously observed for its aristocratic participants – simply did not apply to them. Juvenal des Ursins reveals how, during the siege of Harfleur, the French King Charles VI wanted to introduce archery practice throughout his land in an attempt to combat the power of the English longbow. His noblemen, however, were aghast at the prospect of peasants joining their army and told him that if he tried to put the measure into effect they would depose him. In contrast, Henry made the ordinary soldier feel welcome within his army.

Henry V was building upon the leadership style of his great-grandfather Edward III. Edward not only showed skill in his use of

archers within the army – he could also speak to them directly and motivate them to fight better. In one memorable incident, near Calais in 1350, Edward and a small English force was suddenly confronted by a much larger body of French men-at-arms. The king immediately identified himself to his bowmen, who until then had been unaware he was in their midst. The chronicler Geoffrey le Baker told of the powerful effect of Edward's action: 'He encouraged his men and spoke to them courteously, saying "Do your best archers – I am Edward of Windsor"'. The archers were galvanized by this and with

A detail from the lost tomb of Jean Juvenal des Ursins, one of the French chroniclers of the battle of Agincourt.

the king watching them were keen to make every arrow count. Edward addressed his soldiers 'courteously' – he did not patronize or condescend to them – and he reaped the benefit, as his opponents were quickly put to flight.

Archers played an important role in the armies of Edward III. Jean Froissart remarked pointedly after Crécy: 'I tell you that day the English archers gave great support to their side, *for many said that by their shooting the affair was won*' (my italics). There was now growing awareness of their value. To put it simply, English bowmen were getting a much more positive write-up in the press of the day. Chroniclers started to take note of when the common soldier had done well and to draw people's attention to it. In the English defeat of the Scots at Homildon Hill, in 1402, it was emphatically stated:

Victory was not by the hands of nobles or lords, but by the means of poor men and servants. No lord, knight or esquire took a step until the archers had defeated the enemy.

The ferocity of the arrow storm at Shrewsbury drew admiring comment:

The archers [began] to draw so thick and fast that it seemed to beholders like a thick cloud, for the sun, which at that time was bright and clear, then lost its brightness so thick were the arrows.

The following year, in 1404, it was noted approvingly that the 'common folk' had defeated a French force attacking Dartmouth.

Thus far, this change in social attitudes, though striking, was limited. Rewards were given by Henry IV in appreciation of the royal bowmen at Shrewsbury, but only to their captains, the knights and esquires who commanded their retinues. A memorial brass to Matthew Swetenham, for example, honoured the squire, giving him the epithet of 'bow bearer' to Henry IV. Swetenham was of gentry stock, holding a hunting office in the royal household and able to afford his own armour. Henry V went further. In an unusual and significant act for the times, he gave greater recognition and status to the vast majority of ordinary archers. Whereas Edward III had used a roughly equal proportion of men-at-arms and archers in his armies, on Henry V's 1415 expedition the archers formed at least

Brass to Matthew Swetenham – bow bearer to Henry IV – at Blakesley (Northants).

three-quarters of the whole force. His use of so many archers had more than just a tactical justification. The king could meet these men on their own level and make them feel part of his enterprise. And when the moment of crisis came, these motivational skills paid off handsomely. The French expected Henry's army to disintegrate under the pressure of their onslaught, but it held together and fought as one.

A clue to this rapport with the ordinary combatant lies in Henry's wild youth. The fun-loving prince so memorably caught in Shakespeare's *Henry IV, Part One*, had a firm basis in historical fact – even if his larger than life drinking companion, Jack Falstaff, was the playwright's own invention. Henry V's contemporaries noted with approval that the king dismissed his tavern cronies on taking the throne and then developed the necessary seriousness and maturity to properly govern his people. Henry's banishment of Falstaff at the end of *Henry IV, Part Two*, 'I know thee not old man', carried a powerful symbolic truth: the king had grown up and put his past behind him. As Thomas Walsingham put it, he had transformed into 'another man, zealous for honesty, modesty and gravity'. And this new self-discipline was vital to win the respect of his army. Nevertheless his earlier drinking companionship in the taverns of London – or as Titus Livius put it, such pleasures as 'the licence of a soldier's life permits' – meant he could talk to the ordinary soldier without affectation. Here his use of English is refreshingly direct and surprisingly modern, showing the down-to-earth way he spoke to his men: at Harfleur he called them 'Lads!' and at Agincourt he urged them forward with 'Fellows – let's go!'

The army Henry was recruiting was based on a system known as 'indenture and retaining'. This was an innovation of Edward III's which replaced the earlier practice of raising troops through feudal obligation. Edward had realized that the feudal levy, which limited active service to forty days and sometimes produced poorly equipped troops, was unsuitable for more extensive campaigning in France. The indenture was the document which listed the names of the knights and ordinary soldiers brought in by retinue – fighting men who were retained or supported by their lord. These were the building blocks of the late medieval English army. It was a much more professional arrangement, for the indenture, which specified the number of men-at-arms and archers to be raised in return for a specified daily rate of payment, was legally binding. It ensured that military contingents were up to scratch. Individual retinues could vary in size enormously. Whereas the king's brother, Humphrey duke of Gloucester, was retained to provide 200 men-at-arms and 600 archers, a lowly squire might bring in just three archers. This was a more sophisticated system than that used by the French – who still relied on feudal service – and Henry V supplemented it by recruiting specialist groups of archers from Lancashire and Cheshire.

As Henry's army assembled in August 1415 the king had a clear vision of its purpose, to renew the claim of his great-grandfather Edward III to the throne of France and enforce it through military might. In Shakespeare's *Henry V* he tells his assembled nobles 'We have now no thought in us but France', and Shakespeare's portrayal of the king invading France in pursuit of the justice of his claim is echoed in contemporary sources. This is how Titus Livius put it:

Henry decided to win back the kingdom of France which belonged to him by birthright. First, however, he sought advice in all the schools and universities from men learned in divine and human law whether he might justly and without fear of wrongdoing seek to regain the crown of France by force of arms. The king then sent an embassy to France with instructions to present his claim to a council of the French and, if by any chance the French should refuse him justice, to announce to them that King Henry would come with an army to claim his rights.

These carefully orchestrated preliminaries were important. They followed the medieval notion of a 'just war' – establishing the case that Henry's war was legally and morally justified – and communicating it to the expedition's participants. The message struck home. John Hardyng put the ordinary soldier's understanding of it: the right of English kings to France 'by succession of blood' was clear.

There is no reason to doubt Henry's sincerity. On his deathbed, the king asserted that he had waged war to prosecute his just title to France and obtain his rights. To bring his army together, Henry's task was to make his sense of mission real for his soldiers. As we will see, this is something he undertook throughout the entire Agincourt campaign. But to advance his claim to France Henry had first to draw a line under the civil war of his father's reign, and create a

Putting the past behind him: effigies of Richard II and his queen, Anne of Bohemia, in Westminster Abbey. Henry V reburied the king and created a mood of reconciliation in the country.

mood of reconciliation and hope for the future. He had to be tough in rooting out conspiracy – and Henry showed these qualities admirably in dealing with the Southampton plot, shortly before his expedition set sail – whilst giving the noblemen of families previously disloyal the chance to rally round his flag. Henry achieved this, typically, through powerful symbolic ritual.

There is a perceptive pre-battle moment in Shakespeare's *Henry V*, where the king implores God:

> ... Think not upon the fault
> My father made in compassing the crown.

Henry knew his father had come to the throne through the deposition and likely murder of an anointed king, Richard II. He realized this unresolved issue could hang like a ghastly spectre over the military enterprise he wished to conduct. As a medieval army lined up to fight, its combatants were faced with the possibility of sudden, violent death. Many would try to make their peace with God in any way they could, and sometimes an improvised, soldierly communion sprang up in the ranks, using whatever was to hand: finding three-leafed clovers to represent the Trinity and putting up makeshift wooden crosses. As men prepared themselves for battle, knowing that the outcome might hinge on intangible factors such as luck, misfortune or chance, they would inevitably wonder if their commander might be punished by God for a particular sin or fault.

It was a tribute to both Henry's martial and his human instinct that he anticipated such a scenario and pre-empted it. At the beginning of his reign he reburied Richard II with full reverence in Westminster Abbey. His father had disposed of the unfortunate king, without any ceremony at all, at King's Langley, and Henry was making a strong, visible statement to his realm – he wished to make peace with the past. As Thomas Walsingham put it, Henry venerated the deposed king as much as his own father and for that reason had him 'regally entombed at Westminster'. But Henry did more than that. He managed to transform Richard II from an omen of misfortune into a symbol of blessing. Stories were soon circulating at court – doubtless with the king's encouragement – that the deposed king had foretold a brilliant military future for him, Richard believing that Henry's 'immense soldierly industry' would one day shine throughout the world. Whether founded in truth or not, this powerful legend could only help Henry's military cause.

The task now facing the king was to communicate his cause to the rank-and-file. In a letter written at Southampton by one of the assembling army, a squire named John Cheney, we find him aware of the great enterprise gathering round him, 'the king and all the lords being here', but hastily trying to gather armour and equipment. Cheney was from Drayton Beauchamp in Buckinghamshire. His family had been involved in rebellion and John had only just received a royal pardon. He had real potential as a soldier, being described by contemporaries as 'a man of exceptional strength', but was preoccupied by money worries and trying to raise a small loan from friends. It was hard for him, in these circumstances, to see any bigger picture. Henry needed to inspire men like Cheney to win victory in France.

Henry had the ability to reach out to others and it was founded on one simple truth: he cared about his soldiers. When we look at the organization of the royal army we see this clearly. Ever since his own life had been saved after Shrewsbury, Henry had maintained a strong interest in battlefield surgery. In his preparations for the Agincourt campaign he drew up contracts with two surgeons, Thomas Morstede and William Bradwardine, who were to provide their services for the duration of the campaign. Morstede was a highly skilled practitioner – author of one of our first surgical treatises – and in his will he left a host of surgical instruments and also a suit of armour, a reminder that surgeons could fight as well as tend to the wounded. Significantly, Henry had stipulated that Morstede bring a team of surgeons with him, a most unusual step which would have attracted the notice of the gathering soldiers. Morstede brought twelve additional surgeons, a horse and cart to carry their supplies, extra medicines and an escort of three archers. His colleague William Bradwardine brought another nine surgeons with him. These men were there to minister to the whole army, not just the select, privileged few. The Agincourt expedition was the first English force to be accompanied by a full medical train.

Such provision of care from a military leader was exemplary and the statement of care and protection it makes is striking. A fifteenth-century illuminated manuscript depicted Alexander the Great visiting his wounded soldiers. By sharing his medical resources, Henry attained a similar standard of kindness, and actions like these forged a

The distinctive red-cross banner of St George – prominent in a display of Agincourt banners behind Sir Laurence Olivier in a publicity shot for Henry V.

real unity. Similar skill is seen in the instinctive generosity of another great warrior king, Edward I. In the winter of 1294 Edward's army was besieged in Conwy Castle and running alarmingly short of supplies. The king refused the small quantity of wine that had been kept back for him and instead insisted that it be shared out amongst his troops.

However, a mood of unity within an army depends on something more durable, a structure to bind it together. Henry's choice was stunningly effective – he would make the Christian warrior of the third century, St George, a symbol for all his soldiers. Today we are accustomed to the red cross of St George – the English flag – as a symbol of national identity. But it was only on the Agincourt campaign that St George truly became our national saint. The powerful sense of patriotism is captured by Shakespeare at the end of Henry's rousing speech at Harfleur:

> ... upon this charge
> Cry, 'God for Harry! England and Saint George!'

The banner of St George is seen prominently in the Olivier film, *Henry V*, flying proudly above the English army. This patriotism is based on a real event – the deeply shared experience of all Henry's soldiers in 1415.

When Henry V came to the throne St George was increasingly, but not yet exclusively, associated with English fortunes. The army of Edward I which invaded Scotland carried a banner of the saint and armbands displaying the red cross were given out to some of the troops. Edward III took things further, making St George the patron of his new chivalric body, the Order of the Garter. The power of this is brought out in a memorial brass to one of Edward III's leading captains, Sir Hugh Hastings. Angels carry Sir Hugh's soul heavenward towards a figure of St George, who acts as the soldier's guardian. He is surrounded by eight comrades-in-arms – and these are the king himself and his leading aristocrats. In the words of Dr Matthew Strickland, co-author with Robert Hardy of an excellent new study, *The Great Warbow*, the saint was at this stage associated with 'the creation of an elite military confraternity'. Edward also introduced 'Saint George!' as a formidable English war cry. In one of his letters, the king proudly related a striking feat of arms on the Crécy campaign. Two of his knights defiantly rode up to a well-defended river crossing and uttered a vigorous shout of 'Saint George for Edward!' The French were completely taken aback. The knights then laid about them, killing two of their opponents and wounding many others, before departing at considerable speed. Once again, Henry V built on his illustrious predecessor's achievement, widening the saint's appeal to encompass the entire army – and indeed the whole nation.

Henry achieved this by making St George accessible to everybody. Military ordinances drawn up by the king compelled his men to

Memorial brass to Sir Simon Felbrigg and his wife. Felbrigg had been Richard II's standard bearer; now he joined Henry V's army for the Agincourt campaign. Pieces of his armour are marked with the red cross of St George to invoke the saint's protection in battle.

wear a large red St George's cross, on their front and back, at all times. This was for the purpose of recognition – the king was providing a uniform for his army. Although the ordinances that survive were compiled after the battle, there is good reason to believe that the measures were put into effect on the Agincourt campaign. Soldiers were then encouraged to appeal to St George for his intercession. Henry's chaplain tells us that as the army marched along the River Somme, with morale faltering, the troops sought the protection of 'the blessed Saint George, to mediate for us between God and our poor people'. Henry himself solemnly invoked the help of the saint on the morning of the battle: 'In the name of Almighty God and Saint George, advance banners. Saint George, give us this day your help.'

We see this idea clearly expressed on a memorial brass to one of the Agincourt participants, Sir Simon Felbrigg, who is shown with the cross of St George marked on pieces of his armour fitted to protect his armpits. The red cross was intended not only for recognition but also to summon the protection of the saint in battle.

Henry made such sentiments concrete by ensuring his soldiers not only wore the cross of St George, but saw actual depictions of the saint as often as possible. The household accounts of John Mowbray, the marshal of Henry's army, show what the king had devised. As the army gathered at Southampton Mowbray purchased 'a piece of cloth of gold, sufficient to make a cross, on a trapping bearing the image of Saint George'. And on top of his tent, a huge metal weather-vane was fashioned, again depicting St George. Amidst the army's banners and standards, Henry wanted his men always to be able to see the saint, wherever they looked – and thus feel St George was actually with them. The idea totally succeeded, for so strong was the army's identification with the saint that it was commonly believed he had actually appeared in the sky above them during the battle, encouraging them to victory. This astonishing report is made in a number of our sources. Thomas Elmham related how during the fight 'Saint George was seen fighting on the side of the English'. And another chronicler echoed this belief: St George had helped the English and 'had been seen above, in the air, on the day that they fought'. Whether or not we believe this actually happened is not the point. These stories were credible enough to contemporaries – and showed that the soldiers generally identified with the saint. Their effect on the morale of the army must have been incalculable.

The gratitude felt by Henry and his soldiers was commemorated in the aftermath of their victory when St George was accorded special honour throughout the realm. On Henry's arrival at London Bridge on 23 November 1415 he was met by an armed figure portraying the saint, equipped with helmet, shield and sword, who handed him a victory scroll recording his triumph. It was subsequently declared by churchmen that greater reverence would be shown to St George, now formally acknowledged as England's protecting saint. Adam of Usk tells us that his feast day of 23 April now became a special day, on which all work ceased, and people attended their parish churches in thanksgiving.

The focal point to all this ritual was the banner of St George. A medieval army depended on its banners and standards, not merely for decoration and display, but also as rallying points during battle. Soldiers would look to the men grouped around them to see how well they were fighting. It was always a crisis if a banner went down and a sign of valour if a man recovered it. Henry's ordinances of war made clear the importance of the banner of St George within the army – and to carry it on campaign and during the battle was an exceptional honour. So, as the expedition assembled Henry made a striking gesture, one that had an enormous impact on his men.

Thomas Strickland was a poor squire from Cumbria. He had little land or money and was constantly in debt. As great magnates arrived at Southampton with retinues of hundreds of men, Strickland could scrape together only two men-at-arms and six archers. He was a little-known soldier and Henry had many magnates in his army of proven courage and reputation. Yet Henry bestowed upon Strickland his highest martial favour – the right to bear the banner of St George for the duration of the campaign.

Here it is worth recalling the comment made about the king by the Frenchman, the Monk of Saint-Denis: 'he knew how to exalt the lowly'. Strickland himself never forgot the experience. He later proudly related that he was 'bearer of the banner of Saint George' at Harfleur and Agincourt, and he went on to serve on Henry's later campaigns, witnessed the surrender of Rouen in 1419, and crossed the Channel for the last time in 1430 to see Henry's son, Henry VI, crowned king of England and France at Paris.

Henry V's choice of Strickland was a telling one. The Cumbrian squire who was always broke had fought in the royal army at Shrewsbury and distinguished himself in the battle. Strickland was later rewarded for his 'good services', and another grant, of two fine horses formerly belonging to Henry Percy, suggests he was fighting in the desperate mêlée around the royal standard when Hotspur launched his do-or-die attack. Twelve years later, the king's choice powerfully recalled and paid tribute to the bravery of a relatively humble soldier. In so doing, he sent a strong message to his gathering army: on this campaign, it was courage that mattered, not rank. This was the spirit which bound his men on the challenging road ahead.

Chapter III

Once More unto the Breach

In the summer of 1415 a large English army set sail across the English Channel. Its destination was Normandy and the French port of Harfleur. Henry's first aim was to capture this strongly defended town. The subsequent siege prompted Shakespeare to give us one of our most famous war speeches, with Henry urging on his troops:

> Once more unto the breach, dear friends, once more,
> Or close the wall up with our English dead.
> In peace there's nothing so becomes a man
> As modest stillness and humility:
> But when the blast of war blows in our ears,
> Then imitate the action of the tiger.

This speech evokes age-old truths. Courage and determination are needed for war and to fight well one has to leap forward into action with the energy of the tiger.

One soldier's tigerish enthusiasm was quickly apparent. In the heat of the mid-August sun, close to 12,000 soldiers were disembarking from their ships and marching towards Harfleur. The English landing was several miles north of the medieval town, at a place called Frileuse, and we have a soldier's testimony to bring alive the moment when the army first reached foreign soil. I want to introduce you to the man who made it.

In Shakespeare's *Henry V* we learn that the likeable ruffian, Jack Falstaff, has died broken-hearted after being banished by the new

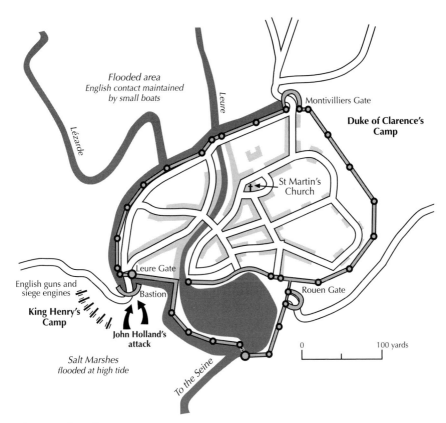

The siege of Harfleur.

king. Henry had to organize his military expedition properly and there was no place for Falstaff's antics. Although the playwright made the character up, he has often been confused with a real-life historical person, the medieval soldier, John Fastolf. The two could not have been more different – and it gives our story a most ironic twist. In the play, Falstaff's death marked a rite of passage and the arrival of manhood and responsible and effective kingship for Henry V. In real life, it was the encounter between Henry and Fastolf which set the tone for the campaign in France.

Fastolf was an ambitious 35-year-old squire from Norfolk. He had been brought up in an aristocratic household and as a 12-year-old gained an insatiable appetite for adventure when, as a humble page, he travelled across Europe in the retinue of Henry Bolingbroke – the

Sir John Fastolf armed for the joust – from a Roll of Arms.

future Henry IV – and ended up on a pilgrimage to Jerusalem. He had learnt his soldierly trade in tough frontier fighting in Ireland, gone on a sea expedition to Flanders and held a military captaincy in Gascony. Now on 14 August 1415, with the great English ships anchoring off the shore, he was first off the small boats, leaping into the water 'up to his sword belt' – as he later proudly recalled. Henry was struck by Fastolf's enthusiasm and decided to draw his soldiers' attention to it. With the landing complete and the army assembled, the king promised Fastolf the first lands conquered in France as a reward. Henry kept his word. In January 1416 it was duly recorded that Fastolf had received the lordship of Frileuse – confiscated from its French owner.

Fastolf's encounter with Henry had lasting impact. He became a stalwart supporter of the war with France, quickly winning his knighthood and devoting his career to a vigorous defence of Henry's conquests. The man who was first out of the boat at Harfleur retired from the fighting with an ample profit – building a fine castle at Caister in Norfolk with the proceeds. But the pursuit of profit was only a small part of Fastolf's undertaking – his writings showed how much he cared, even in retirement, about the great martial enterprise begun by Henry V on the Agincourt campaign. In the mind of this soldier at least, to be honoured by such a king was an unforgettable experience.

Henry and his men were now approaching Harfleur. In the English army were more than 2,000 men-at-arms and nearly 9,000 archers, along with several hundred masons, carpenters and labourers. The heavily defended town was a daunting sight to the ordinary English soldier and Henry's chaplain gives us a striking eye-witness account of it:

> The town is situated at the very end of a valley, on the banks of the river Seine, from which the sea flows in past the middle of the town, ebbing away to a distance of a mile or more. And the fresh-water river, which descends through the middle of the valley, fills the ditches to a good depth and breadth.

The chaplain was struck by the strength of Harfleur's fortifications:

> The town was fortified with high and well-built towers and three gates. And in front of the entrance to every one of these gates, the enemy had constructed a strong defensive work, which we call a barbican.

Harfleur certainly had substantial water defences, for the River Lézarde ran through the town from north to south – its entry and exit points protected by towers and gates – to join the Seine estuary. There were three town gates: the north-eastern could be protected by flooding the river valley; the south-eastern was sheltered by the river. The most vulnerable was the Leure gate, but it was protected by a massive barbican which reached

Caister Castle, Norfolk, built on the proceeds of Fastolf's war spoils in France.

nearly to the height of the walls. The garrison could reach it through a moveable bridge across the moat and then shelter in it and fire at the attackers.

Harfleur was a considerable prize. The port dominated the Seine estuary and it would be an ideal base if the king wished to return to Normandy with an army of conquest. On the present campaign, its capture would allow Henry the military options of striking along the Seine towards Rouen and Paris or towards the English garrison at Calais. Henry had to plan his next move. Harfleur's normal garrison strength was fifty men (thirty-five men-at-arms and fifteen crossbowmen) but 300 extra soldiers had just gained entrance to the town under the leadership of the talented young nobleman Raoul de Gaucourt. The king needed to stop further reinforcements arriving and conclude matters swiftly before an opposing army could be gathered against him, so that his men would not be caught between an ongoing siege and a strong relief force.

The king's brother, Thomas, duke of Clarence, from his tomb effigy at Canterbury Cathedral. Clarence missed Agincourt - one of many invalided home at Harfleur - and later attempted to emulate his brother's achievement but met with disaster at Baugé.

An early 'bombard' or siege gun.

Henry first completed the encirclement of the town. On 18 August his brother, the duke of Clarence, took a force round to the eastern side of Harfleur and established a blockade. The soldiers set to work digging protective trenches around the English war camps, putting up outposts and keeping watch for any French counter-attack. Then the king began to position his cannon – the biggest of which were 12 feet long and 2 feet wide. To be really effective against such impressive fortifications, Henry needed to get them as close to the defences as possible. But pushing the cannon forward carried a real risk, putting them within range of the enemy's own artillery and making them vulnerable to a spoiling raid from the defending garrison.

Henry had recruited more than thirty skilled gunners for the campaign to spearhead his attack, supported by over a hundred labourers. Now the king showed astonishing energy, supervising the construction of gun emplacements, protective trenches and moveable wooden screens, to be raised for a volley of fire and lowered to protect these specialists from the enemy. He was seen urging his men on and advising them on the placement of the cannon. Within a short period of time all was ready and a deafening bombardment commenced.

In Shakespeare's *Henry V*, the chorus introduces us to the king's mighty guns:

> Behold the ordnance on their carriages,
> With fatal mouths gaping on girded Harfleur.

In the Olivier film, the first shot of the siege shows a large cannon being manhandled towards the town's walls. Contemporaries were fascinated and awe-struck by these monsters. The cast-iron guns could launch projectiles weighing up to a quarter of a ton. They gave the largest nicknames: 'London', 'The Messenger', 'The King's Daughter'. Gunners poured tar over the stones – setting them alight, before ramming them down the muzzle – to ignite the timber in the town's fortifications. The Monk of Saint-Denis describes the terrible firing of these 'enormous stones, enveloped in thick clouds of foul smoke', emitting a 'terrifying noise' as if 'vomited from the very jaws of hell'. Their barrage continued day and night. It was the focal point of the siege.

With his guns in action, Henry spread a brutally effective joke to lift the spirits of his troops. The good commander instinctively knows how to communicate with his men and can use simple, down-to-earth imagery to make his point. The particular image used by the king was immortalized by Shakespeare, for early in the play *Henry V* we find that the French have sent a mocking gift of tennis balls, to disparage Henry's claim to the throne of France, suggesting instead that he occupy himself with a little light recreation. Henry's reply is appropriately robust:

> When we have matched our rackets to these balls
> We will, in France, by God's grace play a set.

He then rounds on the Dauphin, the son of the French king Charles VI, whom he believes is behind this flippancy:

> Tell the pleasant Prince this mock of his
> Hath turned his balls to gun stones.

The story is no mere dramatic invention: it is found in a number of contemporary sources: Thomas Elmham confirms that tennis balls were sent to the king before his invasion of France and John Strecche gives us the king's forceful reply: 'I shall play with such balls in the Frenchman's own streets that they will stop joking, and for their mocking game win nothing but grief.'

Timing is everything. The king did not release the details of this episode before the invasion, but waited until his men were already assembled outside Harfleur. Then Henry allowed the story to spread and the gist of it was soon circulating in popular ballads. This was a clever ploy, for now the slighting gesture of the French would anger the entire army. Henry's tough response would raise a laugh in the ranks and lift morale, with the fire from his big guns 'shattering the town itself and its walls', as Adam of Usk noted with grim satisfaction. This was a most effective riposte – as one popular chronicler made clear, Henry had visibly returned the compliment and his soldiers enjoyed seeing it: 'He played at tennis with his hard gun stones'.

These guns were supported by an array of wooden machines, which catapulted projectiles. Henry was concentrating his fire on the massive barbican protecting Harfleur's Leure gate. It was a tough target – but the king knew that if he could win the barbican and place his guns there, the intensity of fire would breach the walls and allow an assault on the town. The garrison performed heroically, blocking up gaps in the walls and repairing their defences. Henry's chaplain was moved to declare: 'I should not be altogether silent in praise of the enemy. They could not in the judgment of men have resisted our attacks with greater determination and skill.'

However, the sheer weight of firepower began to tell. By 16 September the barbican was badly damaged and its masonry disintegrating. With commendable spirit, the garrison sallied out in a surprise attack and destroyed a couple of the English guns. Henry's response was immediate. He launched a counter move, sending an assault party to storm the barbican. Shakespeare rightly emphasizes the power of such a moment:

> Stiffen up the sinews, summon up the blood
> Disguise fair nature with hard-favoured rage …
> Hold hard the breath, and bend up every spirit
> To his full heart. On, on you noblest English …

It was a dangerous assignment, because the soldiers had to fight their way in under fire from French troops manning the nearby town walls. A number of the king's companions expected the command to go to an experienced captain. They were surprised when Henry gave it to a relatively untested nobleman, Sir John Holland, described by the chaplain as 'brave and high spirited, though young'.

This proved to be an inspired choice. Holland's father had lost his lands for supporting rebellion against Henry IV. The new king was giving his successor the chance to restore his family's reputation and regain their estates. Holland now led the assault with considerable élan. He and his men first set fire to the barbican with a volley of flaming arrows and then ran forward and stuffed firebrands through the holes in its walls. Using a clever trick – perhaps suggested by Henry himself – they scattered an inflammable substance (possibly sulphur) to bring up the intensity of the flames, then burst into the stronghold. The French ran back to their inner defences, but these were subjected to the same treatment and the triumphant Holland then raised his banner over the whole fortress to signal victory. The garrison was forced to retreat to the town walls, hastily blocking the Leure gate with timber, stone and earth. But their position was now highly vulnerable.

Onlookers were impressed by Holland's bravery. By giving him the chance to lead the attack, Henry showed astute judgement. The king had taken a risk – but a justified one – in allowing the young aristocrat a chance to win his spurs. Decisions like these were typical of the way he motivated his army.

Holland's success paved the way for Harfleur's surrender. Henry's chaplain surveyed the damage done to the town. Its fine towers had

Effigy of Sir John Holland - with his first and third wives - in the chapel of St Peter ad Vincula, Tower of London. Holland led the successful attack on the barbican at Harfleur and was restored to the family earldom of Huntingdon in 1417 as a reward for his valour.

been 'rendered defenceless' and throughout Harfleur 'very fine edifices, even in the middle of the town, either lay altogether in ruins or were so shaken as to be exceedingly damaged'. On 18 September the French captain Raoul de Gaucourt opened negotiations. He felt the terms offered by Henry were too harsh – and the English in return prepared for an all-out assault. Proclamations were made throughout the army to ready men for the attack and a ferocious bombardment was unleashed. This prompted new discussions, which led to a formal treaty of surrender being agreed on 22 September. The following day Henry entered the town in triumph.

Henry had faced determined resistance from Harfleur's defenders and this angered him. He was a superb military commander but there was a darker side to his personality – excessive severity. The king could be needlessly cruel. Great leaders sometimes have to be ruthless, but this was Henry's Achilles heel. The chronicler Monstrelet caught the harshness of his response:

> The greater part of the townsmen were made prisoner and forced to ransom themselves for large sums, then driven from

A family tragedy: effigy of Michael de la Pole, earl of Suffolk, and his wife, in Wingfield Church (Suffolk). Suffolk died of dysentery at Harfleur. His son – who succeeded to the earldom – was killed at the battle of Agincourt.

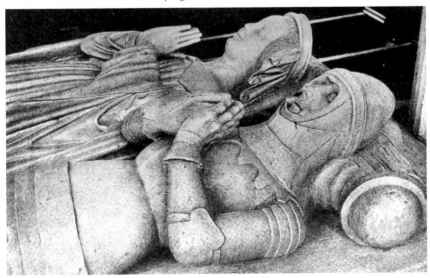

the town with most of the women and children ... It was a pitiful sight to see the misery of these people as they left their town and their belongings behind.

We must be careful not to project our own sensibilities onto the tough realities of medieval warfare. If the besieger felt he had a right to a town, he would be under a moral obligation to protect its inhabitants only if the gates were freely opened to him at the outset. Nevertheless, even within the conventions of the time, observers felt that Henry's behaviour was vindictive. The Monk of Saint-Denis was struck by the peremptory expulsion of 'the sick, the poor and the elderly' and the English commentator Adam of Usk, while appreciative of Henry's achievement, believed the king's interpretation of contemporary laws of war went too far, describing how inhabitants were stripped naked and humiliated, 'with halters and nooses around their necks'. This was an excessive reaction – and clemency would have suited Henry's political purposes much better.

Effigy of Thomas Fitzalan, earl of Arundel, and his wife, in the Fitzalan chapel, Arundel (Sussex). The earl fell ill at Harfleur and died shortly after his return to England. The king felt his loss keenly - Arundel had fought against Glendower's rebels and led a force on Henry's behalf in support of the Burgundians in 1411.

Yet winning Harfleur was a considerable success and Henry soon recovered his equanimity. He wrote a report of the siege to the city of London, expressing his delight in the force of the artillery bombardment and speaking movingly of his confidence in the 'fine power and good diligence' of his soldiers. The king was rightly proud of his men. But their achievement had come at a cost. Soon after the siege began, an alarming outbreak of dysentery had spread amongst Henry's soldiers, striking down some of his leading followers. Strangely, it seems to have been more virulent amongst the aristocracy than the ordinary soldier. But soon it was decimating the army.

This was a most demoralizing event – made conspicuous by the prominent figures in the army either killed or invalided home. The earl of Suffolk died from it, as did Richard Courtenay, the bishop of Norwich. The death of this young clergyman, a personal friend of Henry's, who had been with him at the siege of Aberystwyth eight years earlier, was an ill omen. The earl of Arundel was carried back across the Channel, but passed away in early October. Yet another personal blow to Henry, although less remarked upon, was the death of John Philip of Kidderminster. Philip was no great aristocrat or promising prelate, but his tomb memorial proudly proclaimed that he had been a friend of the king. Henry knew Philip as the nephew of one of his most trusted advisers, Sir Thomas Erpingham and the friendship had come about through Philip's courage as a soldier. He had distinguished himself in the combat at Saint Cloud in 1411 – when a small English force under the earl of Arundel had supported the Burgundian side in the French civil war. Henry had sponsored this expedition. The memorial also recalled Philip had fought with daring and bravery at the siege of Harfleur. The two men's friendship, one a king of England, the other a relatively humble knight, showed once again

Memorial brass to Sir John Philip – described as a friend of the king – at Kidderminster (Worcs).

how Henry could cut across the divide of rank and bring his army together.

The wave of death and sickness hit the expedition hard. Over 1,500 men had to be invalided home in a convoy of boats, and prominent amongst them was the king's own brother, Thomas, duke of Clarence. This was a very real crisis, as Adam of Usk made clear:

> Many died of dysentery during the siege; thousands of others returned home. Some went legitimately, having got permission to do so, while others were invalided home because they were sick, but there were some others who, disgraceful to relate, simply deserted the army.

Henry's chaplain estimated the disease carried off a substantial body of troops, and 'directly afflicted and disabled many of the remainder', so that the army's active strength – once a garrison had been installed at Harfleur – was left at a little less than 6,000 men. But now the king showed his mettle. His physician won fame through his efforts to heal the sick and we find a record of that high standard of care provided in the household accounts of John Mowbray, the marshal of the army. Here was a man close to Henry – responsible for discipline and regulation of the troops – with a remarkable concern for the suffering of his soldiers. The unfortunate Mowbray had been struck down himself, and was soon purchasing medicines for 'the sickness of the flux', and setting up his private toilet – a freshly constructed seated latrine – as the ravages of dysentery set in. Yet he found the time and energy to tend his men and try to prevent the disease spreading. It was believed that infected drinking water might be the culprit and in Mowbray's response we find every detail attended to.

In between sips of 'water plantain' – a sort of medieval castor oil – and visits to the 'privy within his tent' Mowbray made urgent provision for the refreshment of his soldiers, ordering up vast quantities of wine, beer, ale and cider from England. These beverages were carried down to Southampton, loaded into barrels, and brought across to Harfleur, where the valiant Mowbray had assembled an array of measuring bottles for pints, quarts and gallons, and hundreds of flagons, complete with stoppers and belt clasps. Every soldier would have his own drinking flask, regularly filled, to protect him from any contamination of the water supply.

Mowbray was forced to retire home at the end of September but his kindness was remembered long after his departure.

To properly replenish his forces Henry had to take drastic action. Those invalided by the disease were sent home in a flotilla of boats and replacements were found for them. This was a complicated logistical operation. The documentary evidence – most recently and thoroughly studied by Anne Curry – suggests that Henry was able to supplement his army effectively, and build it up to a marching strength, after the garrisoning of Harfleur, of between 8,000 and 9,000 men. If these latest figures are correct, it was a superb feat of organization – one that has important implications for our understanding of the campaign.

Henry's need to gather reinforcements forced him to stay in Harfleur longer than he had anticipated. He had to hold the port and wait for fresh troops to arrive and this left his soldiers at a loose end. As we have heard, some had already deserted, and Henry needed to do something to lift their morale. The king's response was masterly. On 26 September he sent a formal challenge to the Dauphin of France, the 19-year-old son of Charles VI, inviting him to a duel.

By issuing this challenge from 'his town of Harfleur' Henry was throwing down the gauntlet to the French court and making clear a serious wish to give battle. He was also making a joke to cheer up his soldiers. This invitation to man-to-man combat was proclaimed to the English army with mock-theatrical ritual:

> We offer to place our quarrel, at the will of God, between our person and yours ... For it is better for us, cousin, to decide this war between our two persons than to suffer our quarrel to destroy Christianity ... We pray that you may have such anxious desire for it.

Here the banter over tennis balls and gun stones was being resumed with a vengeance. Soldiers were being asked to imagine their lithe, athletic 28-year-old king in armed combat with the slovenly 19-year-old Dauphin, whose lifestyle had long been a cause for scandal. Here is Titus Livius on Henry's physical strength:

> he was marvellously fleet of foot, faster than any dog or arrow. Often he would run with two of his companions in pursuit of

the swiftest of does and he himself would always be the one to catch the creature.

The Dauphin's athletic regime was rather different. Dissolute, fat and sluggish, he normally rose at 4.00 pm and spent the night in a series of drunken debauches. He was so physically unfit that a royal trip across Paris had to be abandoned because he was complaining of exhaustion at the Ile de la Cité. Recently some historians have billed the Dauphin an unjustly maligned political player. But the simple epithet of one Paris citizen who saw him often enough is more to the point: 'wilful, but with little sense'.

Engraved portrait of Charles VI of France.

The challenge caught the popular imagination. A monk of Westminster had the disparity between the two men in mind when he complimented Henry, declaring he was 'not fleshy or burdened with corpulence, but a handsome man, never weary, whether on horseback or on foot'. A more incongruous match could hardly be imagined. There was little danger of the challenge being taken up. But Henry's mock seriousness – the sending of the summons by herald, the number of days he would wait for a response – allowed his men a much-needed belly laugh.

Underneath the humour, a serious point was being made. In the medieval world a nation's ruler not only headed his realm, but his physical condition was also seen as a symbol of the country's ills. The Dauphin was heir to a king who experienced bouts of periodic insanity, when he believed he was made of glass and had to be held together with hoops in case he might break. The failure of either the unstable monarch or his portly offspring to exert authority had led to a terrible civil war between the aristocratic houses of Orléans and Burgundy. Henry was reminding his men that they had a commander up to the task in hand – unlike their adversaries – and that the country they were invading was divided by feud and suspicion. Whatever hardships they had suffered, these circumstances still gave them a remarkable opportunity.

Henry's message to his men – I am willing to risk my own person, and submit to God's judgement, because my cause is right – showed his strength as a leader. Edward III had done the same, sending a provocative letter of challenge to his adversary on 26 July 1340 asking that 'the debate … be conducted by our two bodies'. Henry now followed suit and his soldiers were reminded of the disparity between the English king and his French counterpart. One poignant archival detail bears this out. While Henry was leading the siege of Harfleur, setting out his great guns and bombarding his opponents, his rival, Charles VI of France, had arrived in Rouen. There, despite

Seal of Louis de Guienne – the Dauphin – from a French charter.

Harfleur's appeals for help, he stayed. But he did take one 'martial' action. A librarian from the Louvre presented Charles with a book his royal master had requested. It was full of pictures of guns and siege engines. While Henry enthused his gunners, his rival sat and perused drawings and sketches of the weaponry which was decimating the town right under his nose – as if there was nothing else he could do. The striking contrast between the two kings was hammered home to the English army at every opportunity. It could not fail to lift their spirits.

CHAPTER IV

On the March

On 8 October 1415 Henry and his army left Harfleur and began their march northwards to Calais. The troops were travelling light – on foot, with their equipment packed on horses behind them. Henry's reasons for marching across northern France have given rise to much debate and we need to review his likely motives. A council of war was held shortly before his departure and we might imagine we are with its participants pondering over the next step to take.

Let us hear first hear how military historians have interpreted Henry's march. Alfred Burne, in his influential survey *The Agincourt War*, did not believe the king wanted to fight the French:

> King Henry gave out his desire to meet the French army in battle during the operation, but the steps that he had taken to march 'light' and as speedily as possible to Calais bear the impression of a directly contrary desire.

And John Keegan, in his important study *The Face of Battle*, agreed:

> At a long council of war, held on October 5th, he convinced his followers that they could both appear to seek battle with the French armies, which were known to be gathering, and yet safely out-distance them by a march to the haven of Calais.

This is the general consensus on Henry's campaign. It rests on the following premise: Henry did not have the strength to meet the

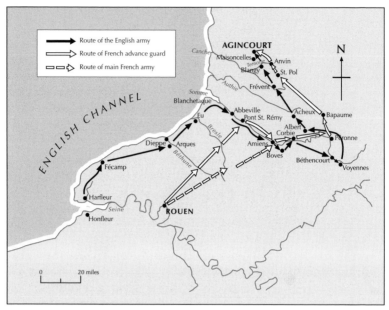

The route of Henry V's army from Harfleur to Agincourt.

French in battle with any realistic chance of success. However, he needed to undertake some action to keep up morale and enthusiasm for the war effort. Simply returning home after the capture of Harfleur was not a feasible option for him – it would have appeared to his countrymen too modest a gain after such a large expedition. His defiant march across French-held territory thus allowed the king to retain his prestige.

If Henry wished to provoke the French, while gambling on his ability to outdistance their armies, it was certainly a risky enterprise. The king's chaplain gives us a glimpse of his preparations. The army was instructed to march light, carrying only eight days' food, and Henry exerted tight discipline over his troops whilst they were on the move, prohibiting any unnecessary plundering which might distract from his men's speed and cohesion and instructing his soldiers that 'under pain of death, no man should burn or lay waste, or take anything save what was necessary for the march'.

We might deduce from this that the English king wished to steal a march on the French and get to Calais ahead of them, and these careful preparations were to achieve this aim. If so, it inevitably affects how we see Henry as a commander. Once we assume

Henry's chief objective was to avoid giving battle, things then go drastically wrong for him. He was unable to get across the Somme as planned because his opponents were on the other side of the river in strength, and as a result he was forced further and further inland. Once he managed to cross the river, he found the road to Calais blocked by a vastly larger army. In this portrayal of the campaign, Henry was outmanoeuvred by his opponents and battle was forced upon him against his wishes. Despite Agincourt's happy outcome, this becomes an indictment of the king's military ability. It suggests that the French lost a battle they should have won and that the debacle at Agincourt was a result of their own overconfidence, rather than the skill of Henry and his soldiers. If we follow this interpretation – which is widely prevalent – we diminish the English achievement. But I want to contest this view.

First, let us consider the broader political and military context. By renewing the claim to the kingdom of France made by his great-grandfather, Edward III, Henry was also reviving expectations of the glory days of campaigning in the fourteenth century. Alfred Burne believed that the plundering expeditions of Edward III's reign influenced Henry in his plan to avoid battle but retain his honour through a dash across French territory:

> If Henry succeeded in his march, he would be reviving the memories of similar *chevauchées* which had done much to raise English prestige in the days of Edward III; he would show that the English army could apparently go where it liked in the lands that he claimed as his own.

However the comparison with Edward III is a double-edged sword. A *chevauchée* was a plundering raid and most of these were leisurely, covering enormous distances. The great raids of Edward's day took months to traverse the length of France, from the Channel ports to Bordeaux. They were designed to gather plunder and inflict damage on the French economy. In the process, English soldiers were given a free rein: columns of troops would fan out, sometimes miles apart, to burn crops and villages and gather vast numbers of cattle. In stark contrast, Henry's chaplain tells us that the king expressly prohibited unlicensed pillaging within his army as they began their rapid march. Rather than evoking the glory days of Edward III, Henry's dash across northern France – if this was all the king ever intended –

would suffer through the contrast with his illustrious predecessor, appearing both hurried and undignified and militarily ineffectual, inflicting little damage on the French.

Recent research undermines Burne's argument, for military historian Clifford Rogers has argued persuasively that Edward III's *chevauchées* often had the aim of provoking the French into battle. This is significant, for if Henry was recalling any specific campaign of Edward's, it was that of 1346–7, where the English army marched through Normandy and Picardy, inflicted defeat upon the French at Crécy and then captured Calais. On 15 August 1346 Edward wrote to his adversary, Philip VI of France, informing him that he was 'making our way towards you, *to make an end to war by battle*' (my emphasis). The English king made clear his determination to fight: 'At whatever hour you approach, you will find us ready to meet you in the field.'

Here important work by Andrew Ayton supports Rogers's argument, showing that the French did not force battle on Edward III at Crécy – with the English king trying to avoid their clutches – but rather, that Crécy was a site Edward was already familiar with and where he had prepared in advance to meet his opponents. Edward III wished to fight on his 1346 campaign and if Henry V was consciously emulating him in 1415, rather than shunning the French army, he would deliberately seek it out.

To get a better understanding of the options open to Henry at the end of September 1415, we need to know how many soldiers were now available to him. The chaplain tells us English numbers were small, with a little under 1,000 men-at-arms and just over 5,000 archers still fit enough to fight, giving Henry a total of some 6,000 men. But other chronicle estimates of Henry's force are higher and Anne Curry, who has made a careful and detailed study of the documentary evidence, thinks that the overall strength of the English army was built up to over 8,000 soldiers. This can be accounted for: although Henry's army had been depleted through dysentery the king used the time at Harfleur to bring in fresh troops and replenish his expedition. In this case, the enterprise was neither rash nor foolhardy and allowed the king to face the enemy and fight.

I believe Henry wanted to take battle to the French. This is not the traditional view but I think several factors support it, the first being the size of the French army gathering at Rouen. Although the evidence here is more patchy than on the English side, valuable new work by Anne Curry shows this army was initially intended to be no more than 9,000 strong. We are used to imagining an enormous French army at Agincourt, and although this view has been challenged, I still believe that a large army was assembled. But a vital refinement needs to be made – initially, French strength was indeed low.

At the beginning of the Agincourt campaign French morale was poor and the trauma of civil war real. The country was divided by faction and from the vantage point of intrigue and suspicion there was little incentive to make a large-scale response to the English threat. Let us consider the viewpoints of the two groups struggling to dominate the court of King Charles VI. In 1414, the Orléanists had regained towns occupied by their opponents and their fear was that if they marched north in strength to counter the English, the Burgundians would simply return by the back door and seize Paris in their absence. At best they intended a limited response to Henry's invasion. From the Burgundian side, the calls to oppose the English were viewed with suspicion. They saw the gathering army as entirely partisan and feared it could be used to expand their rivals' influence in this part of France. When an Orléanist magnate was made captain-general of Picardy soon after the English invasion, the Burgundians refused to accept his authority and deliberately did not co-operate with him.

In short, neither side trusted each other and the army gathering to face Henry V suffered as a result. Charles VI's councillors seem to have decided upon a damage limitation exercise – keeping the main protagonists out of it and recruiting a small but professionally led army.

I suggest here a likely Plan A for Henry – formulated at Harfleur in the last week of September. The king would strengthen his army, raise morale and then march out to seek battle. In this scenario, Henry would face a French army roughly the same size as his but lacking real motivation. It is likely that the king expected this encounter to take place before he crossed the River Somme. French documentary evidence supports this view, for soldiers joining their army were retained to serve 'in the Pays de Caux or elsewhere' – suggesting the parts of eastern Normandy and Picardy between the Rivers Seine and Somme – where a confrontation with the English seemed to be expected. The Norman chronicler Thomas Basin, whose family hailed from the Pays de Caux, emphasized that

Henry's intention in marching into the region was 'to force the French to fight'.

Anne Curry's detailed research into the respective size of the armies in late September 1415 changes our picture of the campaign. If, after the dysentery outbreak, Henry intended a rapid dash across France – avoiding his opponents – it made little sense to wait two extra weeks at Harfleur reinforcing his army. Curry then speculates that these numbers remained roughly the same throughout the campaign, with the English holding their troop strength at above 8,000 men and the French at best recruiting a couple of thousand more. However, I believe that while Henry was building up his army at Harfleur, things on the French side began to change rapidly.

Let us return to the crucial council of war on 5 October. Contemporaries tell us that Henry's plan to march to Calais now faced strong opposition. According to one chronicler 'the majority of the councillors were of the opinion that a decision should be made not to march on', and it was only after Henry vigorously intervened that it was concluded that they 'should pass from Harfleur to Calais, following the overland route'. It used to be thought that their reluctance was caused by the terrible dysentery outbreak. But Anne Curry's new research shows this is unlikely to have been the reason, as strenuous efforts had been made to reinforce the expedition, so we must look for an answer elsewhere.

Henry's chaplain provides valuable detail on what was actually discussed. Most of the council of war believed it would be highly dangerous to send out an army 'daily growing smaller, against the multitude of French, *which constantly growing larger*, would surely enclose them on every side like sheep in folds' (my emphasis).

This powerful testimony warns us against Curry's view that the two armies remained approximately equal in size throughout the campaign. Instead, it alerts us to two important developments. First, the dysentery outbreak had not been contained. By isolating the sick, and sending them home, Henry had hoped to stop the disease spreading, but sadly this had not happened. As a consequence, although the army had been reinforced, its numbers would continue to be depleted by illness as the campaign progressed. Secondly, the French force gathering to oppose them – originally intended to be 9,000 strong – was expanding rapidly. One well-informed observer, the anonymous French chronicler of Charles VI, indicated that the army at Rouen now numbered more than 14,000 men. Burne believed this figure was 'doubtless exaggerated' but Clifford Rogers finds it 'quite credible', noting that the source is a good one. Rogers also points out that the French could expect further reinforcements as battle drew near, whereas the English could not – and this would certainly explain the concern in the English camp.

French enthusiasm for the war, lacking during the siege of Harfleur, was growing fast. A pointer lies in the unfurling of the Oriflamme, the sacred banner used by kings of France at times of great danger to the nation. We should not expect Charles VI to do much banner waving but fortunately a proxy was at hand – Guillaume Martel, lord of Bacqueville – and on 10 September 1415 Martel reverently carried the banner from the Abbey of Saint-Denis, north of Paris – the burial place of the French kings – to Rouen. The arrival of the Oriflamme, the red banner of war, offered an image of patriotism which could transcend the recent political intrigues and evoke the great triumphs of bygone days and the more recent success of Roosebeke in 1382 – a victory won before Charles VI had lapsed into madness. As the Oriflamme was unfurled at the mustering point of the army, and news came through of the courageous if ultimately futile defence of Harfleur, the mood of the country began to change. As fresh recruits rushed in, the French army soon became larger than anyone had anticipated.

This change provoked the difficult council of war, for Henry and his men now realized they were likely to face an army twice their size. One factor remained in their favour: the Burgundians had played no part in the French preparations and with Burgundy neutral the English still had a chance. But Henry had to assert his leadership. He still wanted to confront the enemy and when the council of war assembled he was clear and decisive. Titus Livius catches the steely determination of the king's address to his captains:

I have the spirit of a very strong man more willing to enter all dangers rather than anyone should impugn the reputation of your king. We shall go with the judgment of God … if they try to hinder us, we shall triumph as victors with great pride.

Adam of Usk relates how Henry, 'committing himself to God and the fortunes of the sword … set out bravely like a lion'. For the soldier John Hardyng, the king 'homeward went through France like a man' and another military source confirms the king was still

Effigy of Sir William Philip at Dennington (Suffolk). He accompanied the king on the Agincourt campaign and later became treasurer of the royal household.

ready to fight his enemies. On 7 October, two days after the council-at-war, Henry's lieutenant at Calais, William Bardolf, wrote that he was ready to help by leading 300 soldiers into Picardy, to draw French troops away from the Somme crossing points. His letter made clear that the French were expected to bar the way of Henry's army and that battle was anticipated.

The English marched out of Harfleur with much of their baggage left behind and such stores as necessary carried on the backs of their horses. Henry kept his men dismounted: the choice of an infantry army made it harder to take rapid flight and was thus more suitable for a battle-seeking force. The experienced soldier Sir John Cornwall commanded the vanguard, the king and the duke of Gloucester took the centre and the duke of York and the earl of Oxford the rearguard. The chaplain said they brought food provisions for only eight days, which is usually seen as proof that Henry wanted to get to Calais as fast as possible. However, an alternative reading is possible: that the king wanted to fight the French first and then replenish his army. If Henry was rushing to Calais at full speed, in a hazardous race across enemy territory, he was bringing highly unsuitable luggage for the trip – some of the most precious regalia ever assembled by a king of England. Henry had gathered a stunning array of items for the journey: a precious crown, a sword of state so valuable it was rarely seen, a gold cross set with precious stones, a piece of the True Cross, set amongst rich jewels and an orb used for the coronation ceremony itself.

The risk in carting such precious objects across France was enormous and the king was in fact to lose many of these items when the French plundered his baggage train during the battle of Agincourt. Henry was deeply upset by their loss – and sent some of his French prisoners off to the back-street markets of Paris, promising them a substantial reduction in their ransoms if they could track the lost regalia down. Remarkably, it was all recovered and brought back to the relieved monarch.

The man responsible for organizing the transport of this priceless cargo was probably John Feriby. He had a useful pedigree of service,

Humphrey, duke of Gloucester, Henry V's brother, shared command of the main body of the army on the march. The king probably saved his life at Agincourt.

Sir John Cornwall with his wife Elizabeth Plantagenet – Henry V's aunt – from a window formerly at Ampthill (Beds). Cornwall, an experienced soldier and jouster led the vanguard of the army on the campaign.

having organised supplies for Henry IV's expedition to Scotland in 1400, and three years later, after the battle of Shrewsbury, he was given the important task of moving the royal pavilions, armour and artillery. Henry V recognized his organizational gifts and brought him on the Agincourt expedition. Interestingly, Feriby fell sick from dysentery after the battle – at Merlimont, near Etaples – a reminder that the disease continued to ravage the army throughout the campaign.

I believe that the king was intending to use the regalia for a stunning pre-battle ritual to inspire his troops. We do know that on the morning of Agincourt a procession occurred, when Henry rode along the line in a magnificent suit of armour, speaking to his men, and then, in full public view, solemnly heard mass. Henry then put on a helmet encircled by a gold crown studded with jewels. Titus Livius described the moment: 'The king put on a helmet and placed over it an elegant gold crown, encrusted with various precious gems and with the insignia of the English.'

I believe Henry chose to carry the royal regalia to powerfully motivate his soldiers. This is how one man responded. Thomas

Effigy of Richard de Vere, earl of Oxford, who commanded the rearguard on the march.

Hostell had been badly injured during the siege of Harfleur, losing an eye and breaking a cheekbone after being struck by a crossbow bolt. In this wretched state, he was so inspired by Henry's leadership that he chose to march with him and fight at Agincourt. His wounds could scarcely have healed. Hostell must have believed a momentous battle was likely to take place and did not want to miss it – nothing else would justify someone in such a terrible condition accompanying the army.

The English moved north-east out of Harfleur, taking the coastal route and quickly passing the towns of Fécamp, Arques and Eu.

Henry V in his heraldic surcoat, with the lions of England and the French fleurs de lys. The king wore it on the last stage of the campaign - showing his men that he was ready to fight and their cause was just.

They met only small-scale resistance and the army's rate of march and discipline was good. By 13 October they were advancing towards the Somme and the famous crossing point used by Edward III on the Crécy campaign, the ford at Blanchetaque. In the traditional version, Henry and his men were eager to cross the river and continue towards Calais. When they learnt from a French prisoner that a large French force was on the other side, blocking their passage, it was the first crisis point of the campaign. But I question whether Henry was trying to cross the Somme before the French caught up with him. On the contrary, the chaplain's account suggests that the army was expecting to meet the French in battle before they reached Blanchetaque. The mood of excitement was tangible as reports came in of a large force assembling in front of the Somme crossing. This was the moment of truth – and the chaplain allows us to glimpse the hopes and fears of ordinary soldiers. Some men wondered about the morale of those opposing them and whether the prevailing suspicion of the duke of Burgundy might work to their advantage. All were readying themselves for combat.

Henry had signalled his intentions to the French – deliberately releasing the French prisoners captured at Harfleur before his army left the town. The prisoners were set free on the strict condition that if the king 'was not brought to battle before he reached Calais' they would surrender themselves again. In other words, they were bound to return to Calais if the English were victorious in battle. If Henry was hoping to avoid the French on his march this arrangement would be utterly pointless. The king was once again throwing down the gauntlet. But the anticipated French challenge did not materialize. Instead, there was a most alarming and unexpected development. It emerged that the Burgundians had begun to support the war effort and were holding the Somme towns against the English. Over the next few days Henry's army marched up-river, in the direction of Amiens, still ready to do battle. Basset's Chronicle – a reliable source compiled from the testimony of English soldiers – described how the king halted and drew up his army to meet the French, knighting some of his followers. Jean de Waurin also reported that the English 'arrayed themselves in order of battle on a fine plain'. Finally, when Juvenal des Ursins related the formal French summons to combat, given at Péronne on 20 October, he stressed that at an earlier point the English king 'had decided to wait for the French, *if they were willing to fight with him*' (my emphasis). But although Henry's army lined up for combat, no opponents appeared.

An astonishing change was taking place in France, with a mood of reconciliation sweeping the country, and old rivalries being laid aside. Few could have predicted it, but in an atmosphere of high emotion, Burgundians were rushing to join what was fast becoming a national army of unity. Henry's force was now in terrible danger. It must have been an awful anticlimax for his troops when the anticipated clash failed to materialize. Instead, they encountered a resolutely applied scorched-earth policy. The chronicler Thomas Elmham described a new determination amongst the French as they harried their opponents: 'Everywhere the bridges and causeways were broken by the enemy ... The French devastated farms, vineyards and food supplies.'

English morale began to plummet. As the expedition followed the course of the Somme past Amiens, continuing to find all crossing points held by the French, Henry began to lose control of his army. At the village of Boves, on 16 October, he had to reprimand his soldiers after an unlicensed drinking spree. A day later, a man who had stolen a valuable object from a church was hanged in front of the assembled troops. The soldiers watched in sullen silence. One senses the king's inner turmoil – he had never anticipated such a situation, with the whole of France suddenly united again, and must have wondered whether God had turned against him. For an alarming couple of days, the expedition looked as if it might disintegrate completely. The chaplain tells us how soldiers quite spontaneously flung themselves on their knees and implored God for help as the whole army sank into despair. Shakespeare famously gives Henry a dark night of the soul on the eve of battle. The playwright's instinct was correct, but the occasion was earlier, for this was the real crisis point. For the first time the king appeared out of step with his men.

The soldier's theft of church property has been made famous by Shakespeare – with Bardolph about to be hung for the crime, and Henry rather brusquely pronouncing 'We would have all such offenders so cut off.' Titus Livius gave most detail on the incident:

> The king ordered his host to halt … Those who had committed the sacrilege *were led out throughout the entire army* and hanged on a high tree till dead. The host was then ordered to proceed.

It was sensible to maintain discipline on the march and to respect religious property, and one of Henry's military ordinances specifically prohibited the stealing of church goods and ornaments 'upon pain of death'. But it was a mistake to push the offence under the nose of the soldiers in such a harsh manner. A Roman military maxim – set out by Vegetius – put it well: 'Soldiers are corrected by fear and punishment in camp; on campaign, hope and rewards make them feel better.'

Yet, remarkably, Henry was able to retrieve the situation. A chance to turn things around came at the small Somme town of Corbie on 17 October. Sensing the despondency of their opponents, a force of French cavalry rode out and charged down a group of hapless archers. The sixteenth-century chronicler Holinshed preserved a remarkable vignette of what followed and, although this is a later source, the tone and feel of the military action he describes seems authentic. The marauding French horsemen had captured one of the English battle standards and were triumphantly carrying it back to the town. The king encouraged his men to go after it. The Cheshire squire John Bromley, followed by a small group of soldiers, 'ran eagerly upon the French', hurled himself into their midst and grabbed it back. With Bromley waving the standard aloft, other English soldiers began to pitch in and the French were chased back inside the town. Henry now had an unexpected opportunity to reconnect with his men. The king trusted his gut instinct and seized it – he stopped persecuting his soldiers and started praising them again. Bromley was rewarded with a valuable cash annuity 'for his valiant recovery of the standard at the sharp and bloody skirmish of Corbie' and the mood of despondency began to lift.

Garter stallplate of Sir Thomas Erpingham - Henry V's most experienced military adviser. He had fought for the king's father and grandfather.

General view of the Agincourt battlefield.

'We are but warriors for the working day': the English king meets Mountjoy Herald, from Olivier's *Henry V*.

The 'preparation for battle' scene in Olivier's *Henry V*: the lines of the French army were recreated by figures painted on glass.

Jean le Meingre, Marshal Boucicaut - Henry V's most formidable opponent - from his Book of Hours.

Henry V enters London in triumph - a detail from Adam Kokowski's striking modern mural.

In battle psychology, the course of whole campaigns can depend on moments such as these. Henry's chaplain related a new sense of urgency and vigour in the English camp. Archers were instructed to cut wooden stakes and carry them sharpened as protection against sudden cavalry attack. Henry had probably learnt of the French plan through the interrogation of prisoners. The chaplain related that 'the enemy had appointed companies of horsemen to break the strength of our archers'. He then added that this report was circulated throughout the army. The stakes were to be 6 feet long and to be arranged in formation in front of the archers' position. The sense that Henry had good intelligence and was able to take counter-measures must have been an enormous boost to morale. The army now raced to find an undefended crossing point of the river. On 19 October impromptu causeways were constructed between the small villages of Voyennes and Béthencourt and the English began to move across the Somme. To further lift his men's spirits the king selected a force of 200 bowmen to establish the bridgehead, supported by some 500 men-at-arms. The archers were leading the way – and all units of the army working together. Henry personally supervised the crossing, standing by one of the causeways to encourage his soldiers.

While Henry and his soldiers had been crossing the river, a much larger French force was gathering at Péronne, east of the Somme. The new choice of muster point underlined an ominous reality of the developing campaign: the enemy army was now attracting considerable Burgundian support and would massively outnumber the English. On 20 October French heralds arrived at Henry's camp with a formal summons to battle. The die was cast. Henry's own army had now recovered its sense of unity, even if some of the men were genuinely terrified of the vast force now shadowing their line of march. But their leader had regained his composure and self-belief and this was quickly transmitted to his soldiers. The king would never have planned to fight in such circumstances – yet he was in these circumstances and intended to conduct himself with honour.

It is Shakespeare who wonderfully portrays this moment, as Henry answers the French herald Mountjoy. Once again I believe the playwright instinctively catches the spirit of the king's leadership:

My people are with sickness much enfeebled,
My numbers lessened …
Yet, God before, tell him we will come on,
Though France himself and such another neighbour
Stand in our way …
The sum of all our answer is but this:
We would not seek a battle as we are,
Nor as we are, we say we will not shun it.

Henry's captains knew they were heavily outnumbered and in a desperate position. Titus Livius described the actual scene. The French heralds announced that all the great lords had assembled in their army and then they spoke directly to the English king: 'They will meet thee to fight … and to be revenged of thy conduct'.

All eyes were on Henry – what is striking in this account is how every nuance of the king's reaction was scrutinized by his followers: 'Henry, with courageous spirit, a firm look, without anger, and without his face changing colour, calmly replied, "Be all things according to the will of God"'.

The king had made peace with himself and God and was resolved to face whatever happened with dignity. Bravado would not work in this situation – the stakes were too high. The men around him were now looking for authentic leadership and this is what they got. Henry took command of the situation and spoke with real authority:

When the herald asked him what road he would take, he answered 'Straight to Calais, and if our enemies try to disturb us in our journey, it will not be without the utmost peril. We do not intend to seek them out, but neither shall we in fear of them move more slowly or more quickly than we wish to do.'

The English army now moved north, with a much larger French force on their right flank. Between 21 and 23 October they kept up an impressive marching speed. Many in the army were really frightened but they knew that they were all in this together. There was no going back – and the king drove this simple yet powerful idea home at very opportunity. Since the Somme crossing Henry had been wearing his heraldic surcoat – known as a côte d'armes – over his armour, and he had encouraged others to do the same. On the evening of 23 October Henry improvised an effective symbolic gesture out of pure fatigue. He mistakenly passed the village selected for his night's quarters. But he refused to turn back, telling those around him: 'God would not be pleased if I should turn back now, for I am wearing my côte d'armes'.

In the language of chivalry this made a simple statement. Once a true knight displayed his coat of arms he would never shirk from battle with his enemies: 'In that noble and perilous day, he cannot be disarmed without great reproach to his honour, save in three cases: for victory, for being taken prisoner, or for death.'

Henry and his men did not have long to wait. On the afternoon of 24 October they crossed the River Ternoise at Blangy and their scouts rode up to the ridge ahead. They galloped back, reporting a huge French army was now ahead of them, blocking the road to Calais. Battle was imminent.

Chapter V

The Battle

On the late afternoon of 24 October English troops lined up on the ridge of high ground north of the village of Blangy. In the valley below was a colossal French force and it seemed as if the entire countryside was teeming with men. The phrases used by participants – an 'innumerable host of locusts', 'forests covering the whole of the country' – as if a biblical plague or dark enchantment was about to be visited on the army, reveal the wonder and sheer terror felt by ordinary soldiers as they saw the enemy at last. They were facing an army of overwhelming size and – as every man on that ridge would have sensed – one powerfully motivated to fight.

All eyes were again on Henry as men watched to see how he would respond. Titus Livius remembered the scout who first saw the French being brought to the king in a state of shock, 'with worried face and anxious, gasping breath'. Henry remained absolutely calm:

> without trembling or showing any anger he set spurs to his horse and rushed to see the approaching enemy. Once he had seen and obtained knowledge of the army, which was too large to be counted, he returned to his men … steady and unflinching.

An English army had held this ground before. For three days, 6-8 November 1355, Edward III had waited with his troops on the same spot to give battle to the French. They had not come. But now the enemy had arrived in force and Henry made what provision he

The power of the crown: Henry V from an engraving of a portrait in Queen's College, Oxford.

could. He took advice from his most experienced captains and chose a suitable deployment for his men. Titus Livius recalled the captains being properly briefed – the king drew up his men 'distributing to each leader the order and place of battle'. But battle was not to be waged that day. The French did not repeat the tactics of Crécy, where they had launched a series of attacks in the early evening on the English position and then fought on, even in the moonlight. Instead they marched north, camping between the villages of Agincourt and Tramecourt, and blocking the road to Calais. Henry followed them, setting up his own camp at Maisoncelles, about half a mile to the south. He had good cause to be wary, for as night fell a picked body of French cavalry launched a surprise flanking raid on a group of archers. This was designed to unsettle the English army but the king remained unflustered and ordered silence to be kept throughout his camp for the duration of the night, so that his soldiers could hear any further movement of the enemy.

There was much to concentrate Henry's mind. Around midnight, as Thomas Elmham recalled, the king sent 'some valiant knights by moonlight to examine the field'. His scouts would have reported on the likely battlefield. It was raining heavily and the ground towards Agincourt and Tramecourt, bordered by woods on either side, was already a muddy quagmire. The French decision to retire from Blangy suggested that they would now choose to fight a defensive battle and wait for the English to advance on them. If the enemy held their position, Henry and his tired and hungry army would have to do precisely this – the last thing the king wanted. If this was not worrying enough, Henry also had to attend to the morale of his soldiers. He knew they had witnessed the size of the army facing them and felt its keen determination – many would now be deeply afraid.

Agincourt has been endlessly discussed in terms of military tactics and these factors are seen as determining both the developing shape of the battle and its outcome. The English longbow was used to such great effect, with the French seeming to take no account of its power, that this feature is obviously both important and fascinating. As a result, the psychology of battle – the less easily quantifiable, yet vital factors of morale, motivation and inspirational leadership – has received far less emphasis. Yet I believe it is crucial and from it all else flowed. If we are able to make a connection with the state of mind of the participants, everything will fall into place. I want to take you down this road. I believe that Agincourt was fundamentally a clash of contrasting emotions. Once we can make sense of them, we will find the unfolding battle entirely different from the traditional account.

To do this we have to understand how Henry motivated his men. This has been a theme developed during the course of the book – but what the king did in the next few hours would be vital. Shakespeare allows Henry to express this perfectly: 'All things are ready if our minds be so'. I want to share with you how I believe the king transformed the mood of his army.

The rituals of preparation performed by commanders are often instinctive and thus do not fall into set patterns. But we are not on the battlefield with Henry and his soldiers, and for us to try and imagine what this might have been like, some sort of structure will be important. It was generally recognized that the king did something very special. Shakespeare made this idea famous, showing the king doing the rounds the night before battle, talking to his soldiers:

> ... who will behold
> The royal captain of this ruined band
> Walking from watch to watch, from tent to tent ...
> For forth he goes and visits all his host ...
> And calls them brothers, friends and countrymen.

This was certainly a characteristic action of the king. During the siege of Harfleur men noted how Henry often chose to walk amidst his war camp at night, chatting to his soldiers. The chronicler Thomas Elmham said something significant had happened before battle – the king had given courage to his men. Titus Livius spoke of a rousing exhortation: 'Be brave in heart and fight with all your might'. But the most impressive tributes were from the French. As they were reluctant to praise Henry – for obvious reasons – it is striking that here they chose to do so nonetheless. The Monk of Saint-Denis described how the king urged his men 'to be mindful of the valour of their ancestors' at Crécy and Poitiers:

> and rather than being scared of doing business with so many princes and barons, be of firm hope that their large numbers will turn, as in the past, to their shame and eternal confusion.

Juvenal des Ursins gave a quite remarkable tribute. Henry urged his followers to be 'good men in battle and do their duty'. He also 'inspired them', and 'boosted their courage enormously'. The message had reached the whole of the army: 'His words were received with enthusiasm, and not only by the leading men; for the common soldiers also promised to fight to the death.'

When Shakespeare shows us Henry mingling with his men – 'a little touch of Harry in the night' – and then, in his St Crispin's Day address, transforming his army's fears and doubts, he captures a fundamental truth about the battle. To explore it, I want to weld the fragments and snippets preserved by the contemporary chroniclers into a coherent whole. The Roman military writer Vegetius expressed a timeless truth: 'An army gains its courage and fighting spirit from the advice and encouragement of its general.' If the precise detail of what Henry said to his men and how he put it across remains unknowable, it is possible, nevertheless, to catch something of its content and to sense its power.

There is a modernity, even a radicalism, about Henry's approach to his soldiers – the way he valued them, reached and understood them, and hence was able to inspire them – which strikes me very much. I have therefore set out how I believe this happened in a modern way – Henry's five steps. These reveal a psychological strategy common to all effective battle ritual: a sequence of actions whose effect is cumulative.

Get the army angry – not frightened

Henry needed to be honest with his men – for everyone knew the situation was desperate. A rumour was going round that the king might be trying to cut a deal with the French and he needed to meet that concern head on and reassure his soldiers. But he also needed to quickly change the mood of his army. As Shakespeare put it:

> Tis true that we are in great danger
> The greater therefore should our courage be.

Fear is contagious and amongst soldiers it can spread particularly quickly. In its worst form – absolute terror – it can paralyse men's will and sap the resolve of an army. Henry's chaplain, who often allows us to glimpse of the feelings of the ordinary soldier, tells us that men were really frightened. Yet Henry enabled them to overcome their fear by turning it to anger. Vegetius warned the commander to look out for fear in his men – in their facial expressions, language and gestures. Once discovered, it was vital to get them angry instead: 'Say anything by which the soldiers' minds may be provoked to hatred of their adversaries, by rousing their anger and indignation.'

Henry instinctively understood Vegetius' advice. He used the arrogance of their opponents to stir a fury which overcame their anxieties. The English were keeping relatively quiet so the sounds of the enemy camp would be easily overheard, and men would inevitably listen, and wonder what their opponents might be doing. Some chroniclers related French boasts that they would mutilate captured archers, cutting off their hands or fingers, or auction them for a derisory sum of money. Such alleged boasts were almost certainly circulating in the English war camp and Henry spoke of them directly when addressing his men.

Henry V also cleverly reminded his troops that this was the eve of the martyrdom of Sts Crispin and Crispinian, thus recalling the massacre of the English bowmen at Soissons in 1414. Likewise, they could expect no quarter from the enemy. Thomas Walsingham told how the threat of death or mutilation at French hands spread quickly through the ranks and men put their fear behind them. English soldiers, 'hot with indignation ... forgot all their misfortunes, exhaustion and weakness'. Anger now fired up the army: 'our men were much excited to rage, *and took heart, encouraging one another*' (my emphasis).

Once the king had got the archers angry, he needed to keep that anger directed towards the enemy. There was a risk that his archers, once roused, might turn their fury towards aristocrats in their own army. For noblemen, as the bowmen knew, would be ransomed if taken prisoner, while they themselves were more likely to be put to the sword. Stories circulating were therefore at pains to show the French treating everyone with equal contempt. The enemy was apparently painting a wagon to haul the captive English king back to Paris and gambling for who would own the most aristocratic prisoners. As the chaplain said disapprovingly: 'It was said they thought themselves so sure of us that night, that they cast dice for our king and his nobles.'

Henry wanted his men to know that they were all in this together – that all were running the same level of risk. His army was thus united in its anger at the arrogance of the French.

Our cause is just

The king then reminded his soldiers, in clear and simple terms, that his cause was lawful and just. The dignity of his claim was emphasized through parading the regalia in front of his soldiers. The visual impact of this would have been enormous – with men catching a glimpse of a sword 'so valuable it was rarely seen', or the orb used during the coronation ceremony. The excitement would be akin to the crown jewels being opened to public gaze for the first time – and there is a point to the comparison, for the last relic of this pre-battle ritual can be seen in the Imperial State Crown displayed at the Tower of London. Although the crown itself was made in 1937 for the coronation of George VI, it contains a pear-shaped red jewel, known as the 'Black Prince's Ruby'. This was believed to have been given to the prince by Dom Pedro of Castile as a token of gratitude for his victory at Najera and subsequently worn by Henry V in the circlet crown, welded to his helmet, at Agincourt.

I am prepared to die for it

Henry told his soldiers he would rather be killed than taken prisoner – he would never burden his countrymen with the payment of his ransom. He made a pledge in front of his men: 'As I am true king and knight, this day England shall never pay ransom for me.' To show this was more than mere bravado he then donned the helmet with the richly jewelled battle crown. This made him a conspicuous target. A body of eighteen French knights swore when the armies met they would knock it off Henry's head or die in the attempt. In the event, they did indeed get close – they knocked a hole in his helmet, breaking off part of the crown and smashing one of its rubies. This was leadership from the front and the troops got the message. They called out in loyalty and real affection: 'Sir, we pray God give you a good life, and the victory over your enemies.'

Leadership through personal example is incredibly powerful. During the battle of Poitiers in 1356 the exhausted army of the Black Prince discovered a fresh division of Frenchmen advancing on them. One of the Black Prince's followers cursed the fact that many soldiers had been sent from the army to guard English Gascony at the beginning of the campaign. How they were needed now!

Henry V wearing a crowned helmet, from 'The Beauchamp Pageant'.

'You lie, you fool!' answered the Prince, 'and speak the worst slander, if you say that I would be defeated and yet still alive.' The force of this declaration – 'If I don't win I will at least die in the attempt' – united his men behind him. The line held and the English went on to secure a remarkable victory.

Henry's resolve inspired his men. The duke of York now begged the king that he be placed in the front ranks of the army – where the risk of death was greatest. A London chronicler, recalling Henry's oath to his men, also set down their moving response: 'We would rather die on this earth than flee.'

We can achieve something extraordinary

Henry then offered his men a vision – that they were destined to be brought together for this battle, to achieve something truly memorable. This was the stroke of genius in his reply to Sir Walter Hungerford that the chaplain recorded for posterity: 'I would not, even if I could, increase my number by one. For those I have are the people of God.'

This of course was the genesis of Shakespeare's memorable St Crispin's Day speech. But at Agincourt itself Henry genuinely created a band of brothers. The gift of a great leader is the ability to turn a disadvantage into a source of inspiration. An eye-witness source remembered the king telling his men:

> They should remember they were born in the realm of England, where their fathers and mothers, wives and children now dwelt – therefore they ought to strive to return there with great glory and fame.

According to Thomas Elmham, Henry now invoked the memory of Edward III and the Black Prince and their triumphs against the odds. By drawing on the 'military memory' of Crécy and Poitiers, the king showed that success was achievable. English armies had done it before. His soldiers were reminded of the love and support of the nation as they prepared to fight: 'Now is a good time, for all England is praying for us. Therefore be of good cheer and go into battle.'

Give the battle to God

The French were seen as puffed up with pride. The Dominican friar John Bromyard, whose writings were an important influence on

Henry, warned of such worldly arrogance before battle. He had singled out in contrast a historical example: Charlemagne's careful spiritual preparation before going into combat. Charlemagne would always hear mass before battle and if he achieved victory, he 'took no credit for it – but rendered thanks to God'. Henry followed Bromyard's teaching. He now encouraged his men to throw themselves and the battle's outcome on the mercy of God. Henry heard mass in front of his soldiers and then made the sign of the cross, 'thus giving courage to his men', as Thomas Elmham related.

Then priests were commanded to come up before the army and pray continually:

> Remember us, O Lord! Our enemies are gathered together and boast in their might. Scatter their strength and disperse them, that there is none other that fighteth for us, but only thou, O God.

The battleground itself was consecrated and the poet Lydgate caught the moment: 'The king kneeled down, Englishmen on every side, and thrice kissed the ground, saying "Christ, as I am thy knight, this day save me for England's sake"'. Then all the soldiers fell to their knees, made the sign of the cross on the ground with their hands, placed their lips on the earth and kissed it, and then took a piece of soil in their mouths. The preparation for combat was complete. Henry had taken a great deal of care over his men and it yielded a handsome dividend, for observers were struck by the unity and cohesion his troops displayed in battle.

But now let us gauge the mood in the French war camp. Here too men were strongly motivated, but as a result of a high-octane adrenalin rush rather than thorough emotional and spiritual preparation. The gathering together of so many former enemies – Burgundian and Orléanist – had created an overwhelming sense of euphoria. Euphoria is heady and exciting. It is not, however, a reliable basis for cool-headed decision-making in a life-or-death situation. One chronicler caught the intoxicating atmosphere well:

> Some of them kissed and put their arms around each other's necks in making peace, and it was moving to see this. All troubles and discords which had been between them, and

which they had in the past, were changed into great feelings of love.

The French had united against the common invader and these feelings were strong enough to dictate the shape of the battle. The atmosphere was exceptionally volatile, as a mood of reconciliation

Chivalric decoration was highly stylized: Anthony, duke of Brabant – younger brother of the duke of Burgundy – from his armorial. In reality, he arrived late at the battle with no time to put on his armour or surcoat – unrecognized, he was killed in the fighting.

swept the country and more and more people rushed to join the army, arriving from all directions. It was now a matter of honour to participate and no one wanted to be left out. The duke of Brabant (the youngest brother of the duke of Burgundy) turned up mid-battle, travelling at such speed that his servants were unable to catch him up and give him his armour or his heraldic surcoat. Bertrand de Blois, riding ahead of the duke of Brittany's contingent, clattered into Amiens at 3.00 am on 24 October, woke up a sleepy town sergeant, and demanded he be led to the French army without any delay. Even the most seasoned veterans became quite swept away with it all. The duke of Alençon, 'who until then had enjoyed a great reputation for wisdom', was supposed to be commanding the second French division, but he abandoned his post and plunged into the mêlée, 'carried away by a foolish passion and by an overwhelming desire to fight'.

These were the two armies assembled to face each other. On the morning of 25 October Henry V brought his men out from the village of Maisoncelles and lined them at the top of a slight ridge. On either side was woodland, which surrounded the villages of Agincourt to their left and Tramecourt to their right, and crucially for what was to come, funnelled towards the English position. The field ahead was virtually flat and about 1,000 yards ahead of them was the French army, barring the road to Calais.

The king drew up his men as effectively as he could. He placed the majority of his archers on his flanks, probably interspersed with clusters of bowmen among his line of dismounted men-at-arms. The archers hammered their protective stakes into the ground – 6 feet long, and sharpened at both ends. These stakes were very much a novelty in Anglo-French warfare and must have given a further morale boost to the English – a 'secret weapon' against the feared enemy cavalry. Armies normally marched and fought in three divisions, but Henry had to put his men-at-arms, who probably numbered about one and a half thousand, in a single line, 'in view of his want of numbers', as the chaplain bluntly put it. There was no reserve.

Men were still being lost to dysentery – and according to Thomas Walsingham many had been surviving on drinking water for days before the battle – so we can only guess at the exact total of the English army. I have chosen to follow the calculation of Thomas Elmham, estimating it had been reduced to around 7,000 men.

Fifteenth-century crossbowman. Marshal Boucicaut's original battle plan envisaged a role for the French crossbowmen – but in the actual fight they were pushed to the rear.

English longbowman, drawn from 'The Beauchamp Pageant'. Most archers at Agincourt wore far less protective armour.

Ahead of them were the French. I doubt if their exact number was known even to them. A number of chroniclers (the Monk of Saint-Denis, Thomas Basin and the anonymous chronicler of Charles VI) believed their force was around four times the size of the English army, and the strong consensus that Henry was heavily outnumbered is well-sourced and founded. I will give the French a notional strength of around 28,000 men. The French heavily outnumbered the English in men-at-arms – the chronicler of Ruisseauville said that here they held a 10:1 advantage. If we allow for at least a thousand mounted men-at-arms, posted on either flank, there would be around 14,000 of them dismounted in the first two

Brass of Thomas, Lord Camoys, at Trotton (Sussex). Camoys – an able soldier, who had fought against Scots, Welsh and French in Henry IV's reign – commanded the English left wing at Agincourt.

French divisions. Behind them in the third line were the lighter armed combatants (known as the *gros valets*), many of whom had horses and reasonable military equipment, and the crossbowmen.

Henry had ridden along his battle line to maintain the morale of his men and presumably his lords and captains did likewise amongst their own retinues. The king would hold the centre, with the experienced soldier Thomas Lord Camoys and the duke of York to the left and right. Now he watched the French in front of him. Earlier in the campaign he had expected to meet a smaller army close to the crossing point of the Somme at Blanchetaque, commanded by the renowned crusader Marshal Boucicaut.

The seal of Jean le Meingre, Marshal Boucicaut.
Boucicaut – a warrior of international renown –
did not hold an overall command at the battle
and the French paid the penalty.

Boucicaut's original battle plan survives, showing the French intended to go on the offensive with a carefully co-ordinated assault: their cavalry would be on the wings – one unit would tackle the English archers, the other would circle the English position and attack from the rear – while the fire of the crossbowmen would weaken the English men-at-arms in the centre. Finally, the French men-at-arms would advance to break the English line and finish the job. By the time he reached Corbie, when Henry ordered his archers to sharpen stakes and carry them with them on the march, the king had probably got wind of this plan. But it had become redundant. With the arrival of so many French princes of blood, there was no longer a clear command structure. Elements of the battle plan may have lingered on: the flank attacks and that on the English baggage train in the rear. But the forest of banners in their crammed first division told its own story. The French now wanted to destroy Henry's army in a mêlée, a heavyweight slugging match between dismounted men-at-arms.

The French had pushed their crossbowmen to the rear. There was still some cavalry on the flanks but their huge vanguard occupied most of the space ahead. It was crammed with aristocrats. Their squires and servants were also pushed to the rear, along with the crossbowmen. The vanguard and the division following it, both dismounted, would consist entirely of noblemen. As the chronicler Pierre Cochon said frankly:

The French thought that they would carry the day because of their great numbers, and in their arrogance had proclaimed that only those who were noble should go into battle.

As he surveyed the fevered press of Frenchmen ahead of him, Henry grasped the possibilities opening up for him. Without opposing crossbowmen, or a really strong cavalry presence, he could use his archers to their best effect. The French had no overall commander – neither the king nor the Dauphin was present and most of their chief aristocrats were in the vanguard, leaving other parts of the army virtually leaderless. The Monk of Saint-Denis described the situation with wry humour:

> Each of the leaders claimed for himself the honour of leading the vanguard. This led to a considerable debate and so that there could be some agreement, they came to the rather unfortunate conclusion that they should all place themselves in the front line.

Their appearance, however, was still daunting. The French plan was simple and was to be carried through on sheer instinct. The cavalry would distract the archers and the main body of men-at-arms would assail the English line with the force of a battering ram. According to Titus Livius, this line of English men-at-arms was no more than four men deep. Against them the opposing French were more than thirty men deep. Yet numbers are not everything. In the rush to action, no French commander saw that in these cramped conditions, and on the muddy ground, such strength might not be the advantage it seemed. But Henry did see this.

These French noblemen were fired up by the aristocratic code of honour and were resolved to smash through the English position, which looked alarmingly fragile. Their numerical superiority meant they could afford to sustain considerable casualties and the English arrow storm, however effective, could only operate for a limited period of time. Each bowman would have two sheaves – totalling forty-eight arrows. Allowing for some reserves, kept in wagons behind the archers' positions, and brought up by the pages as the fighting commenced, the arrow storm could only maintain its full intensity for around twelve minutes or so. With careful aim, a good archer could loose at least seven or eight arrows a minute. It was likely that the volleys would be carefully controlled – the psychological impact of massed, co-ordinated shooting would be far more terrifying than 'firing at will'. But when the French men-at-arms reached the English position the archers would have to fight hand-to-hand with the more heavily armoured and better equipped men-at-arms in the desperate combat which would follow.

Henry saw that he had to make the battlefield terrain work for him. The ground was waterlogged and the mud heavy and clinging. This was crucial – for as Thomas Walsingham related, because of the softness of the ground, 'it was extremely difficult to stand or

The traditional view of the battle of Agincourt.

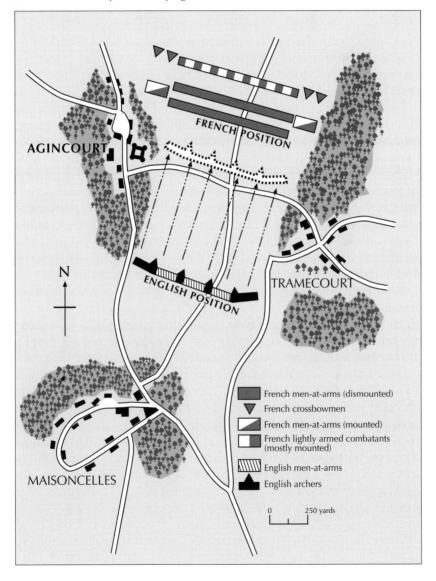

advance'. The chronicler Pierre Cochon told how men-at-arms 'sank into it by at least a foot'; for the Monk of Saint-Denis it was 'up to their knees'. Juvenal des Ursins made it clear that men 'could scarcely move their legs and pull them out of the ground'. In such terrible conditions, it was vital that the French be made to do the work and attack the English position. But initially, they showed no sign of doing this. They were content to adopt a defensive position, knowing full well the English were tired, hungry and short of provisions and could not wait there indefinitely. For two hours the armies surveyed each other across the muddy battlefield. Henry had prepared his men well but he knew a long delay would start to sap their spirits. The king needed to begin the action.

This is critical. There has, until now, been only one way of describing how Agincourt commenced and our whole understanding of the battle is based on this interpretation. It runs as follows: Henry, after consultation with his senior captains, gave the order for the army to advance. The defensive stakes, which protected the archers' positions, were then pulled up and the whole English army began to move across the battlefield. They continued their advance until they were at extreme bowshot range – at between two and three hundred yards from the French army. Then the English stopped, reformed their line and the archers hammered their stakes back in. They then put the French troops under intense arrow fire and after a short interval, first the French cavalry, and then the infantry, moved forward to attack them.

This substantial English advance on the French position was first suggested by Sir John Woodford, who did valuable research on the battlefield site in the aftermath of another famous victory – Waterloo – and mapped Agincourt in 1818. His version of events was followed by Henry V's biographer, Charles Kingsford, at the beginning of the twentieth century, and further developed by Alfred Burne some fifty years later with his theory of Inherent Military Probability. Burne sought out a tactical factor and built his reconstruction around it. His depiction of how Agincourt began was incorporated in all subsequent accounts and here is how Christopher Allmand summed it up in his 1992 biography of Henry V:

Slowly the army advanced the better part of 700 yards, stopping some 200 yards short of the enemy, now within range of the

English arrows. There the archers drove into the ground the stakes, which each had been ordered to cut some days before. *It was from this second position that the English were to fight the battle.* At a range of some 200 yards the English began to rain arrows upon the French. (My emphasis.)

All the sources do indeed confirm that Henry V ordered his army to advance. Its march to longbow range allows us to explain a comment of Jean de Waurin, followed by Monstrelet, which is otherwise not easy to understand:

Straightaway the English approached the French. First the archers began with all their might to shoot volleys of arrows against the French for as long as they could pull the bow.

Burne's account is therefore superficially plausible. Once Henry decided to move forward, he needed to reach a position where he could dictate the battle, and setting up a new line for his army within bow range fitted the bill.

But there is a fundamental problem here: knee-deep in mud, how long would it take the English to advance and set up their second line? Their manoeuvre would expose them dreadfully. Clifford Rogers has estimated it would take soldiers twenty minutes to cover 450 yards of Agincourt's rain-soaked fields, and thus over half an hour to reach the new line – and then they would have to hammer in their stakes. The English were a sitting target for the French cavalrymen the entire time, giving their opponents plenty of notice of their intentions and the chance to launch their attack while the archers were without protection. So why didn't they? Matthew Strickland has recently acknowledged this serious problem with the accepted version:

This was a dangerous manoeuvre, for it meant they had to abandon the defensive positions on which they were so reliant and that for the moment the stakes carried by the archers would be of no protection; if the French cavalry units were to launch a sudden charge at this critical moment, all might be lost. These few hundred yards must have seemed interminable, but the French still made no move.

The more I thought about this, the less sense it made. Since the French had cavalry forces on the wings and plenty of time to use them when the English were vulnerable, why would they obligingly wait until the archers got within bow range, then allow them time to hammer in their stakes and start firing before launching their charge? The traditional scenario is quite unbelievable.

We need to remember the terrible state of the battlefield for, as Christopher Allmand rightly said, 'the condition of the ground assumed great importance'. Torrents of rain had turned it into a quagmire. Yet it was the French who seemed to suffer from this, despite having to cover far less distance than their opponents. As the Monk of Saint-Denis put it: 'they were already overcome with fatigue before they reached the English'. And the anonymous chronicler of Charles VI added that, whereas the French were exhausted, 'the English were fresh and unwearied *as they had not moved from their advantageous position*' (my emphasis). This contradicts the accepted account of an English advance 700 yards forward.

There is another way of understanding Henry's order to advance. I believe it can be understood in terms of battle psychology and ritual provocation. The English undertook a limited, but energetic move forward, seeking in this way to provoke the French into charging at them. Most surprisingly of all, the tactics they used were borrowed from hunting practice rather than any military manual. I have selected what I call the five features of this audacious ploy.

The ambush

The chronicler Monstrelet gives us most detail on this:

> The king of England sent about 200 archers behind his army so that they would not be spotted by the French. They secretly entered a meadow near Tramecourt, quite close to the rearguard of the French, and held themselves secretly there *until it was time to shoot*. (My emphasis.)

Juvenal des Ursins confirmed that there was an ambush placed in one of the woods on the flank of the French position. One contemporary observer, Jean Le Fèvre, felt compelled to investigate the story, but said there was nothing to it. However, Matthew Strickland finds it quite believable:

There is a hint here that some regarded this as something of an underhand ruse, but there seems little reason to doubt the essential plausibility of Henry's attempt to offset the great odds against him by the use of surprise.

Henry probably knew of similar surprises in famous battles of the fourteenth century – the sudden attack behind the French third line at Poitiers and its imitation in the victory of Sir John Hawkwood at the battle of Castagnaro in 1387. These had made a crucial difference to each battle's outcome. But in the traditional version of the battle of Agincourt, it is unclear what this 'surprise' was supposed to achieve. It would have been suicidal for the hidden archers to spur the French into an attack while the English line was still struggling forward through the mud to get into its second position, less than 300 yards from the French line. But once the English line had reformed, all its bowmen would able to hit the enemy and fire from the ambush would make little additional impact. Only by reframing the action and understanding Henry's real tactic does the ploy of concealing the archers make sense. The archer ambush was intended to provoke a reaction.

The stakes

We have assumed up to now that, once the English began to advance, the stakes, which had been knocked into the ground to protect them, must have been pulled out again and dragged forward to the new position. But the sources are unclear on this and difficult to interpret. Titus Livius put the fixing of stakes after the order to advance. However, the chaplain said the stakes were set into position and the advance followed later. He makes no clear reference to a repositioning of the stake wall. It would not have been easy to do this quickly when knee-deep in heavy mud. The Monk of Saint-Denis commented on the novelty of archers carrying lead-covered mallets – in other words, it was necessary for them to hammer the stakes into the ground. And one anonymous source, known by historians as the pseudo-Elmham, said that they were left behind when the archers moved forward: 'The archers, *leaving behind them in the field their sharp stakes*, which they had before prepared in case of meeting the French horsemen' (my emphasis).

As the stakes clearly served an important military purpose, it would be surprising if they were abandoned at a distance of some

700 yards from the reformed English line. But there is another possibility: the archers might have employed a trick – moving out a little way from the stakes, screening them from view, and then when the French cavalry charged, dropping back behind them again. This manoeuvre would ensure the archers remained protected. It had been used in an earlier battle, at Nicopolis in 1396, when the Turks put a screen of troops ahead of a row of thickly planted stakes, thereby hiding them from the French horsemen. The renowned French crusader Marshal Boucicaut was fighting on the opposing side and military historian Matthew Bennett has plausibly suggested Henry learnt about this ploy from a book written about the marshal's deeds.

However, there is a problem with this idea that needs to be addressed. The chaplain related that French scouts had discovered the position of the stake wall and warned their army of it – and this seems to rule out the possibility of any trick being effective. Matthew Strickland has suggested a way of resolving the issue, one that also allows us to incorporate the apparently conflicting testimony of Titus Livius. If some of the archers had indeed carried stakes on the advance, and replanted them further forward, but left the bulk of the wall intact behind them – they could have then fallen back, surprising the French cavalry: 'The French could well have been tricked into thinking the English had abandoned all their field defences'.

Boucicaut had been the architect of the original French battle plan, which intended to use cavalry attacks to bring down the English archers and Henry had ordered his men to carry sharpened stakes as a response to this threat. The stake wall, screened by archers, set up a trap for the French horsemen, rather like the concealed nets used by huntsmen to bring down deer in a forest. One of the chief English aristocrats, Edward, duke of York, had indeed compiled a hunting treatise, called *The Master of the Game*. York's expertise in hunting is significant, for one version of the Brut chronicle believed it was he who suggested to the king that every archer use stakes against the enemy.

The signal

Sir Thomas Erpingham was in his late fifties and was Henry's most experienced military adviser. He had campaigned with the king's grandfather, John of Gaunt, and had been a stalwart supporter of his father, Henry IV. Monstrelet brought out this aspect – 'a knight grown grey with age and honour' – and there is a pleasing piece of banter in Shakespeare's play between Erpingham and the king at the battle camp at Agincourt, which catches the real respect and affection Henry V felt for him. After the earl of Norfolk returned home with dysentery, Erpingham had become marshal of the army. He was tough and reliable and a good man to have in a crisis, so Henry gave him responsibility for the deployment of the archers on the morning of battle. Shortly before the advance, Erpingham rode

Detail of a statue of Sir Thomas Erpingham, now on the Erpingham Gate at Norwich. Henry V had the wisdom to seek and take advice from his most senior captains.

Erpingham Gate, Norwich.

along the English line and threw his marshal's baton high in the air. After this dramatic gesture he then shouted a word rendered by foreign chroniclers as 'Nestrocque!' – usually thought to be 'Now strike!' or 'Knee stretch!', an order for the archers to fire. If this was what he shouted, it is puzzling since the English bowmen were still well out of range of their opponents.

Erpingham's command may actually have been '*Menée* stroke!', the order to blow the 'stroke' or horn call known as the *menée*. In *The Master of the Game* the duke of York made it clear that this was the call used for hunting deer. Remarkably, this hunting signal was now being transferred to the battlefield.

The Church of St Mary the Virgin at Erpingham (Norfolk). Sir Thomas built the perpendicular tower – which spelt out his name in stone on its battlements - after his return from Agincourt.

The hunting cry

Erpingham's gesture prompted a vigorous noise from the troops, who now started to move forward. The noise they made is usually described as a war cry – which seems logical enough, as the army was starting its advance. But to many chroniclers the extraordinary din was more like a braying pack. The chronicler of Ruisseauville used words like 'huer', 'braier' and 'crier', indicating a cacophony

The Agincourt battlefield as seen from the Agincourt-Tramecourt road.

of odd and alarming noises – braying, honking and chanting. These were the sounds of the hunt. For centuries, in times of peace, unemployed archers had taken to the woods with their bows to hunt deer. They would await the oncoming animals, while the game was driven towards them by beaters – who raised a clamour to drive the creatures forward.

Hunting had long been regarded as a good training for war. After the battle of Poitiers the Black Prince escorted the captive French king, John II, from the south coast of England to London. As they passed through a forest, 500 men suddenly appeared, bearing bows and arrows, swords and shields. The French king was amazed. The Black Prince told him: 'they were men of England, foresters ... and it was their custom each day to be thus arrayed'. Matthew Strickland describes this shamelessly stage-managed event as a piece of 'chivalric sport': the image being conveyed to the French is that England is a country full of hardy bowmen, living rough, but ready to follow the Black Prince back to France should he so command.

The experience of hunting is important, for the word used by a number of French chroniclers, 'huer', has a specific meaning: 'to shout while hunting', a vocal imitation of the hunting horn. Jean de Waurin and Jean Le Fèvre – both present at the battle – described the English making a 'grand hué'. In 1327, during the Wearsdale campaign, the chronicler Jean Le Bel told how English archers taunted Hainaulter men-at-arms with the hunting cry of 'Hahay, Hahay!' – the cry used to drive deer towards the nets.

I believe the violent din – described by the pseudo-Elmham as a noise 'which penetrated the heavens' – was the prearranged signal

The battle of Agincourt reinterpreted.

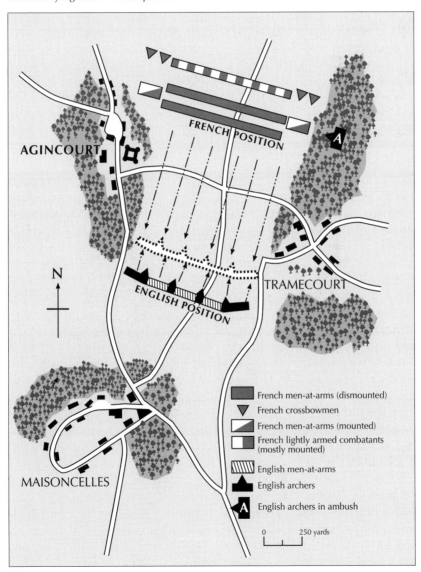

for the archers hidden in the woods by Tramecourt to start firing at the French, in order to goad them forward. Monstrelet said that, as the English moved forward with a great cry, 'the hidden archers also raised a great shout and began shooting hard and fast at the French'. At the same time, the English army, which had noisily advanced some ten or twenty yards, began to taunt their opponents. The hunting cries were deliberately provocative – as were the banners displaying the French royal coat of arms alongside the English, which were impudently waved in their direction. The archers – so disparaged by the aristocrats opposing them – now brayed and shouted as if they were pursuing a pack of animals. For a moment the French were dumbfounded by such blatant cheek. The English cry 'was a cause of great amazement', as Monstrelet put it.

The French response

The provocation worked. Many of the chroniclers tell us that the French now reacted quickly. The chaplain said that when Henry began to advance towards the enemy, 'the enemy, too, advanced towards him' and added that 'men-at-arms from each side advanced towards one another'. This is very different from the traditional account of inexplicable French delay. The pseudo-Elmham is quite specific: when the English moved forward a distance of only twenty paces 'the enemy now first stirred himself'. Thomas Walsingham also believed that when the English began to move forward, the French 'considered the moment was favourable to attack'. One version of the Brut chronicle noted when the command 'Advance banners!' was given to the English army, 'then the French came rushing down, as if to ride over our men'; another that when the English started to advance, '*immediately* trumpets sounded, and the French came galloping down'. Similarly, the Monk of Saint-Denis observed that, when the English started to march forward, '*at almost the same moment* the French advanced against the enemy' (my emphasis). It is worth repeating how the anonymous chronicler of Charles VI stressed that the French 'were exhausted by their advance', whereas 'the English were fresh and unwearied, as they had not moved from their advantageous position'. I believe that once Henry had provoked the French, he then held his line and waited to receive them. Then, as the French surged towards him, they came under intense arrow fire.

The English archers prepare for battle, as reconstructed in the 1944 film, Henry V.

Two final details are significant. At the start of battle the French cavalry units were seriously undermanned. It was said that many of the horsemen had wandered off during the long wait and could not be found again. Yet if the English army had slowly crossed the heavy field of Agincourt, there would have been ample warning of their approach and plenty of time for the French to find those who had drifted away and gather their forces together. I think a sudden and most surprising act of provocation better explains why more horsemen were not at their posts.

Also, as the English began their advance, Henry ordered up his baggage train to protect the rear of the army from possible cavalry attack. According to the chaplain, some of these wagons were plundered by the enemy before they could get into position. It is unclear who robbed the baggage – but if it was indeed the French horsemen, it is easy to imagine their angry response to the archers' mockery. In the traditional version it is harder to envisage, for the wagons would be in place long before the cavalry attacks started.

All the sources do agree that the battle started with a cavalry charge on the English archers and that things quickly went wrong

Archers prepare to shoot, again as portrayed in Henry V.

for the French. The units of horsemen were under-strength and had not picked up much momentum on the heavy ground. They now rode into a devastating arrow storm. Some turned back; others forced their way on, only to collide with the stake wall. The chaplain put it simply: 'many were stopped by the stakes driven into the ground'. According to Jean Le Fèvre, the leader of one of the mounted contingents, William de Saveuse, had his horse brought down by one of the stakes and was killed as he lay on the ground.

Some horsemen fled straight into the path of their own advancing vanguard, which was now struggling through the clinging mud. Then the dismounted men-at-arms came within range of the English bowmen. Men bowed their heads under the sheer weight of the

A reconstruction of the English archers' viewpoint, from Henry V.

The village of Agincourt as seen from the battlefield. The medieval castle stood just to the left of the church.

arrow storm. The French were sustaining heavy casualties but kept pushing forward. As they closed in they switched formation from line abreast to three columns, 'to break through our strongest points and reach the standards', as the chaplain grimly related. This seems to have been an intentional manoeuvre – and if so, was an extraordinary feat, given the hail of arrows and the heaviness of the ground. The shock of the impact pushed back the English line: 'In the mêlée of spears which then followed, they hurled themselves against our men in such a fierce charge as to force them back almost a spear's length.'

This was the crisis point. The French wanted to bring down the English banners, kill the commanders fighting under them and then punch their way through the line. In the ferocious onslaught which followed, the duke of York and the young earl of Suffolk were both slain. French knights now converged on the king's own standard.

Leadership from the front: Henry V protects one of his brothers from the enemy, as depicted in James Doyle's Chronicles of England *(1864).*

Roger Vaughan's effigy at Bredwardine (Herefordshire). Vaughan and his father-in-law Daffyd ap Llewelyn (Davy Gam) may well have died saving the king's life.

Henry showed astonishing courage, wielding a battle axe and trading blows with the enemy. When his brother, the duke of Gloucester, was wounded and dragged towards the French, the king

Effigy in Abergavenny Church to William ap Thomas – a Welsh squire who took part in the battle. Henry's rapport with soldiers he had fought with in Wales may have saved him at Agincourt.

stood over his body and fought them off. Ordinary soldiers pitched in to protect him. Later tradition had it that one of them, the Welshman Daffyd ap Llewelyn, known by his soldiers' nickname of Davy Gam, died saving the king's life – and Llewelyn's story lay behind the creation of Shakespeare's memorable Welsh soldier Fluellen. The legend may have some truth in it, for contemporary sources told of Henry knighting two men during the battle – the other was Roger Vaughan, Llewelyn's son-in-law, who also died in the fighting – and such a gesture was reserved for acts of outstanding valour.

Seeing the fierce fighting around their leader, the archers now resolved to join the fight: 'when their arrows were all used up, seizing axes, stakes, swords and spear heads that were lying about'. This was a crucial moment. It took enormous courage for the archers to leave the protection of the stakes and enter the mêlée. If the French men-at-arms reorganized themselves and turned on them they would be annihilated. But their sudden intervention took their opponents by surprise. They hacked and stabbed at the advancing Frenchmen and kept attacking, pushing further and further into the mass of the enemy, 'acting together and with great energy' as Monstrelet recalled. Jean de Waurin paid tribute to their determination: 'They struck whenever they saw breaks in the line.'

Henry's pre-battle motivation of his men now paid off handsomely. The Monk of Saint-Denis believed the English 'were fighting with so much passion as they knew that for them it was a matter of life and death'. Titus Livius told of a mood of ferocious determination sweeping the army: 'the English were unusually eager to kill – for it seemed there was no hope of safety except in victory'. The English archers' lightness and mobility gave them an advantage over the heavily armoured French men-at-arms and the mallets used for hammering in the stakes became a handy impromptu weapon. In increasingly cramped conditions, as they advanced into the narrowing funnel of ground, the French line began to recoil in disarray. This was the moment Henry had been waiting for and he now pushed his men-at-arms forward. The whole English army was fighting with remarkable discipline and cohesion and the battle began to turn in their favour.

The French men-at-arms felt the force of their advance suddenly slacken. Instead of pushing into the English, they began to collide with each other, floundering and falling in the mud. The squires and servants who might have helped them recover their footing had all been sent to the rear. Now men asphyxiated under the sheer weight of numbers. A terrible pile of bodies built up around the English banners, with Henry's men clambering over the top to strike fresh blows against the now demoralized enemy. French overconfidence gave way to ghastly panic. The chaplain remembered how 'fear and trembling seized them … there were some who that day surrendered more than ten times'. Whereas the English, sensing victory was within their grasp, now found fresh reserves of strength. Something truly remarkable was happening – the cold, exhausted, hungry army was fighting with stupendous power. The chaplain paid moving tribute to soldiers who had lost all fear and were dauntless in combat: 'Nor, it seemed to our older men, had Englishmen ever fallen upon their enemies more boldly or fearlessly, *or with a better will*' (my emphasis). The fight degenerated into a rout.

Yet there was to be a last, terrible event. Henry had heard that his baggage train had been attacked and plundered and now a third line of French appeared to be lining up for a charge. His men were distracted, busily capturing French noblemen. The king feared that his small force might, even at this late moment, still be overwhelmed. He ordered that the enemy prisoners be killed in cold blood. It was an awful decision to have to make.

This incident is understandably shocking to us and was seen as terrible by Henry's contemporaries. Jean de Waurin put it bluntly: 'all those French noblemen were decapitated and inhumanly mutilated there in cold blood'. Waurin also made clear that many of Henry's soldiers were reluctant to carry out his command – not out of moral scruple, but because they did not want to lose the ransom money for their prisoners:

When the king heard this, he ordered a man and two hundred archers to go into the host to ensure that the prisoners, whoever they were, should be killed. The esquire, without refusing or delaying for a moment, went to accomplish his sovereign master's will.

Brass to Sir John Bernard at Isleham (Cambs). He was one of the knights told to kill the French prisoners.

But we must place this decision within the realities of medieval warfare. An army composed of dismounted men-at-arms could not keep formation and collect prisoners at the same time. As a result, soldiers were prohibited from taking prisoners until an order or signal was given, signifying victory was certain. During the battle of Crécy one of Edward III's German allies came to the king and said:

> 'Sire, we wonder greatly that you permit the shedding of so much noble blood: for if you were to take them alive, you could thereby make great progress in your war, and would gain very great ransoms from them'. And the king responded that they should not marvel at it, for thus it had been ordered, and thus it had to be.

The situation at Agincourt was much the same. As Titus Livius recalled, 'The English took no prisoners until victory was certain and apparent.' Crucially, Henry's order was in response to French efforts to restart a battle that had seemed finished. The Monk of Saint-Denis suggested that these men were trying to get out of the way, not attack the English, but other sources told a different story. According to Jean de Waurin, many had regrouped, 'showing signs of wanting to fight, marching forward in battle order'. Their standards and banners were unfurled – showing that battle was to recommence. Titus Livius described what happened next:

> The king sent heralds to the French of the new army, asking whether they would come to fight or would leave the field, informing them that if they did not withdraw, or came to battle, all of the prisoners, and any of them who might be captured, would be killed without mercy.

Detail from Henry V's ordinances of war concerning prisoners. They could be a source of great profit but capturing them distracted soldiers. It was forbidden to take them before a signal that the battle was won.

This was 'a moment of very great danger' as Jean de Waurin emphasized. The French third line posed a very real threat. They had been joined by men-at-arms from the failed cavalry attacks and the chronicler of Ruisseauville declared that these remaining French soldiers were of sufficient strength to take on Henry's army: 'they might have fought well against the English and all their power'. The king had to do something. If the French made a determined attack at this late stage, with the archers away from their stakes and mostly out of arrows, the men-at-arms exhausted by the fight and many soldiers preoccupied by taking prisoners, they would have stood a real chance of success.

Military command sometimes requires really tough decisions. This was one of the hardest Henry would ever face. The king broke chivalric convention by killing prisoners but even French chroniclers understood the reason, and did not blame him for it. Significantly, they criticized instead the Frenchmen who had rallied the third line. This is a fine example of how the story of a battle

William Bruges – one of the heralds present at Agincourt, afterwards identifying those slain in the battle.

is always told in the winners' favour. Had the French succeeded, they would have been admired for their determined resistance when all seemed lost, while Henry would have been censured for failing to anticipate their actions.

When Henry put this drastic measure into effect the French third line hesitated – and then slowly began to drift away. When the threat had passed, the killing order was rescinded and the remaining prisoners – and there seem to have been well over a thousand of them – were then spared. Now at last it was all over. A French herald told the king that the day was his. He had won an incredible victory and for a moment Henry was at a loss for words. Then he looked over to the woods on his left and asked for the name of the castle he saw. It was Agincourt. Monstrelet recorded the king's memorable reply:

> Then, as all battles shall bear the name of the fortress nearest to the field on which they are fought, this shall for ever be called the Battle of Agincourt.

CHAPTER VI

The Legacy

It is fascinating to be writing a guide to Agincourt at a time when the battle is once again the subject of national debate. It is not often in such discussions that I find myself on the side of the traditionalists! I have been most interested by the recent work of Anne Curry, who argues that Agincourt was not the victory of the underdog that has long been celebrated, and that the armies were roughly the same size. The contrast between Curry's view of the battle and my own is most apparent in her view that, overall, Henry V 'displayed a lack of confidence because he was afraid of failure'. I think that both the king and his soldiers would have found all this surprising.

With the battle of Agincourt over, Henry called his soldiers around him and spoke to them simply and informally. The Monk of Saint-Denis caught the moment, telling how the king

> assembled his victorious troops and, after making a sign that they should all be silent, thanked them for having so bravely risked their lives in his service and encouraged them to preserve a memory of that brilliant success. He also urged them not to attribute their victory to their own strengths but to accord all the merit to the special grace of God, *who had delivered into their small company such a great multitude of the French* and had brought low the latter's insolence and pride. (My emphasis.)

As the chronicler Thomas Elmham put it, it was a battle where 'the smaller army overcame the many thousand'. Henry's informality

King Henry's empathy with the ordinary combatant was echoed, centuries later, by Lord Nelson's concern for his men. Significantly, this Georgian bust of Henry V was owned by Nelson – it is now in the Jerusalem Chamber, Westminster Abbey.

was a mark of his confidence – a commander who urges his men forward with 'Fellows, let's go!' has a ready authority that is quickly communicated to his soldiers. Christopher Allmand, in his 1992 biography, saw Henry as 'a natural commander of men, confident in himself, able to inspire others'.

It was indeed the victory of the few against the many – recent historical revisionism notwithstanding – and the disparity between the two armies made the result utterly devastating for the French. Here is how the chronicler Pierre Cochon saw it: 'The ugliest and most wretched event that had happened to France over the last thousand years.' And the Monk of Saint-Denis was inconsolable: 'O eternal dishonour! O disaster for ever to be deplored!'

The French nation was distraught and a year after the battle the poet Alain Chartier summed up the mood in his *Book of the Four Ladies*. The plot is heart-rending: in the aftermath of Agincourt four ladies debate who is the most unhappy – the husband of one has perished in battle, another has been taken prisoner, a third is missing in action and a fourth has fled shamefully. English losses were relatively light – at most around a hundred, the most prominent of whom were the duke of York and the young earl of Suffolk, whose father had died at Harfleur – whereas thousands of their opponents had been slain. Henry's chaplain gives us a vivid and appalling picture of how the French casualties piled up in the closing stages of the battle:

the living fell on top of the dead, and others falling on top of the living were killed as well … such a great heap grew of the slain

Detail of the effigy of Sir Robert Waterton at Methley (Yorks). Waterton was one of the guardians of the duke of Orléans during his long period of English captivity.

and of those lying crushed in between that our men climbed up those heaps, which had risen above a man's height, and butchered their enemies down below.

The grim picture painted by the chaplain is confirmed by a chronicler from Ruisseauville, just north of the battle site, who spoke of five grave pits hurriedly dug, each containing 1,200 Frenchmen, and topped with a wooden cross. And then there were the prisoners: heading the list were the dukes of Orléans and Bourbon, three counts and the unfortunate Marshal Boucicaut. Like so many others, Orléans had arrived at the last minute, only deciding to join the army on 17 October and hurriedly purchasing extra armour and warhorses en route. He had plenty of time to reflect on his hasty

Charles, duke of Orléans, imprisoned in the Tower of London, shown several times in this fifteenth-century miniature.

Armorial of Ghilbert de Lannoy – a lucky survivor of the French catastrophe.

decision – regaining his freedom only in 1440, nearly twenty-five years after the battle. The duke of Alençon should have joined him in captivity. He had been fighting fiercely in the mêlée around Henry – and may have dented the king's helmet. Suddenly surrounded by English troops, the duke attempted to surrender – but a frenzied soldier struck him down: a sign of the savagery of the combat around the royal standard.

The luckiest survivor was Ghilbert de Lannoy. Lannoy, twice wounded, had been shut up in a barn with ten other equally helpless captives. This suggests that Henry was sending prisoners – under escort – some way behind the lines. When the terrible order to kill the captives was given the building was set on fire. Incredibly, Lannoy managed to drag himself out on all fours just in time to escape the blaze. One of Henry's most prominent captains, Sir John Cornwall, then appeared, but fortunately the killing order had now been rescinded and a relieved Lannoy went into captivity instead. Lannoy, who was an experienced soldier, understood why the awful decision had been taken and did not hold it against Henry. He later went to the Holy Land on the king's instruction, compiling a detailed survey of routes to the city of Jerusalem.

Medieval society measured a battle's worth by the high-ranking prisoners taken, along with lists compiled by the heralds of all the leading noblemen slain. But as the English army marched back to Calais it rejoiced in the courage shown by its leader. He fought 'not so much as a king but as a knight' said Thomas Walsingham admiringly and the line from the Agincourt Carol – 'In Agincourt field he fought manly' – was sung out with pride by his troops. The battle had a particularly powerful effect on one soldier. Before the campaign John Cheney had been worried about money. After it, 'animated by ardent faith', he spent several years travelling the Holy Land where fittingly, his most celebrated deed was the slaying of 'a huge, savage giant'. Henry would have approved of the exploit.

Agincourt gave Henry V an international reputation. The joyous celebration in the city of London on 23 November 1415 was followed by a visit to the capital, some six months later, of the Holy Roman Emperor Sigismund – who, according to the delighted chaplain, 'gloried in the exploits of our king'. In 1417 Henry invaded Normandy with a fresh army and within two years had conquered it. 'The time of worship [honour] for young men is now', wrote one delighted soldier. The martial adventures of Sir William Bourchier, one of the heroes of Agincourt, were avidly followed by his wife Anne, writing to her friend the prior of Llanthony, near Gloucester, she told him of her pride in his 'great prowess'.

The astonishing success continued. In May 1420 Henry V of England was made regent of France by the Treaty of Troyes, which disinherited Charles VI's son, the Dauphin Charles, younger brother of the portly Louis. (Louis himself had died shortly after his challenge to a duel by the English king – perhaps out of shock, or so it was said.) The treaty was celebrated by the famous marriage alliance between Henry and Charles's daughter Katherine of Valois. Henry now held Paris and much of northern France and enjoyed the support of the duke of Burgundy. But the king was struck down in the prime of his life, succumbing to illness and dying at Vincennes on 31 August 1422.

Charles VI died shortly afterwards, leaving Henry V's baby son – Henry VI – king of England and France, with his uncle, John duke of Bedford acting as regent of France. However, many French aristocrats refused to accept the Treaty of Troyes and supported Charles VI's disinherited son – Charles VII – in setting up an alternative kingdom, centred on the city of Bourges and the region of the Loire. Once again there were two claimants to the throne, and the English would have to enforce their rights through further conquests.

For a while their fortunes prospered. Bedford was an able administrator – and he was supported by the gifted military commander, Thomas Montagu, earl of Salisbury. The two of them won a stunning victory against the French, and their allies the Scots, at Verneuil on 17 August 1424. Verneuil has been rightly dubbed 'a second Agincourt'. Again, powerful pre-battle ritual and devotion to St George was used to motivate the army. The French had brought in new, heavily armoured cavalry from Milan, and these Lombard horsemen were as devastating as the cavalry at Agincourt had been useless. The English archers could make little headway against their high-quality armour and the horsemen crashed through the entire English line. But the archers picked themselves up and joined the men-at-arms with a great shout. The revitalized army took the battle to their opponents – and won. All men who had fought in the English army – archers and men-at-arms – were rewarded with land. The wonderful sense of unity that had been born at Agincourt reached its fruition at Verneuil and together these two battles consolidated England's military reputation. Its standing army was now rightly regarded as the best in Europe.

Disaster struck four years later. The earl of Salisbury was hit by a chance cannon ball at the siege of Orléans and died of his wounds. He was a genuine war hero and the English nation was devastated. An army under Joan of Arc subsequently relieved the city and defeated the English at Patay. Shortly afterwards Charles VII was crowned at Reims. Little by little, England lost her French possessions. By 1450 Normandy had fallen; by 1453 Gascony had gone as well – leaving Calais as the last English outpost in France.

Yet Agincourt was remembered long after enthusiasm for Henry's war in France had diminished. The king had wanted the battle to be properly commemorated. On the eve of his invasion of Normandy, in 1417, he decreed that anyone who had worn a heraldic surcoat at the battle had the right to bear a coat of arms. This royal act needs clarification. All the great lords on Henry's expedition were entitled to a coat of arms anyway, along with about 80 knights and perhaps 1,200 squires who had fought for the king. But surcoats also seem to have been distributed along the line before the battle. Henry was choosing to extend the honour to ordinary soldiers – making clear that nobility could also be won through participation in the fight. Some took up the offer and the special clause for 'the men who, with the king, bore arms at the battle of Agincourt' recognized the bond forged between them – they were a real band of brothers.

One man determined to perpetuate the memory was the king's brother, Humphrey duke of Gloucester. Gloucester commissioned a life of Henry V by the Italian humanist Titus Livius, who was able to draw on Gloucester's own recollections of the battle. He described the moment when the duke was wounded by a sword blow and fell to the ground:

The king himself now put his feet astride the legs of Humphrey – for the renowned duke fell with his head against the king's feet but with his feet to the enemy. In this position the king fought most courageously for a long time so that his brother might be carried safely from the enemy to his own men.

Sixty years later, in 1475, it was ordinary soldiers – now marching with Edward IV's army in northern France, and passing close to Agincourt, who paid tribute to the great battle in their letters home. In 1513 King Henry VIII, about to go to war in France himself, commissioned an English life – Titus Livius had written his in Latin – of the victor of Agincourt and sought to emulate him in that campaign. The English garrison at Calais always marked the anniversary of the battle: 'going in procession, praising God, shooting guns, with the noise and melody of trumpets and other instruments'. By the mid-Tudor period both Henry V's courage and the quality of his leadership at the battle were firmly remembered. Edward Hall recalled Henry's defiant address to his troops before Agincourt: 'England shall never pay ransom, nor Frenchmen

The myth: Laurence Oliv
poses as the effigy of Her
V in the 1944 film Henry

The reality: the remains of the king's actual effigy in Westminster Abbey.

triumph over me, for this day by famous death or glorious victory, I will obtain honour and fame.'

In 1592, just seven years before Shakespeare's *Henry V*, John Stow wrote in his *Annals of England* of Henry's exploits. He 'never failed his men' and 'fought with his enemies with an ardent heart'. And his men responded strongly to his leadership. As the popular refrain – the 'Bowman's Glory' – put it:

Agincourt, Agincourt!
Know ye not Agincourt?
Never to be forgot
Or known to no men?
Where English cloth yard arrows
Killed the French like tame sparrows,
Slain by our bowmen.

Agincourt's story is still recalled at times of war or crisis. A story circulated that a force of ghostly archers had been seen fighting for the British army at Mons in 1914. R B Mowat, who significantly published a short biography of Henry V shortly after the First World War, was struck by the king's bravery, good fellowship and determination. The 'astonishing victory' at Agincourt 'permanently established his reputation as a general and made him the most famous soldier in Europe'. The Second World War of course created the Olivier film version of Shakespeare's play. Shortly after the war ended E F Jacob wrote: 'It is as a soldier that Henry V can be seen at his best, determined to win his just rights and fully confident of his ability to do so.'

I firmly believe that the campaign and battle of Agincourt stand as testimony to Henry's skill. He did not try to avoid giving battle to the French, and when circumstances changed in a way he could hardly have foreseen, he held his army together and motivated it to fight. The outcome was quite astonishing. Henry V was a natural leader. He understood the science of war and the language of medieval European chivalry – even if, at moments of crisis, he put necessity first. But his exceptional qualities were timeless: outstanding courage, a brilliant military instinct and remarkable empathy with his men. The best commanders make do with what they have and can conjure something extraordinary out of nothing.

Henry had no idea where or when he would be fighting until shortly before Agincourt commenced. But his improvised use of Sts Crispin and Crispinian was a stroke of genius. He stoked the fires of ordinary soldiers' anger before the battle – the opposing French saw them as expendable, just like their hapless fellows at Soissons – and honoured their contribution after it. His men responded with bravery, discipline and determination and fully deserved their astonishing victory. Shakespeare was right:

> This story shall the good man teach his son
> And Crispin Crispian shall ne'er go by,
> From this day to the ending of the world,
> But we in it shall be remembered.

CHAPTER VII

The Battlefield Today

I have spent many years guiding people around battlefields, and I strongly believe that seeing the actual site allows us to make a real connection with powerful past events which can remain remote on the printed page. The battle location is a gateway to the strong and contrasting emotions of combat: terror, exhilaration, panic and remarkable courage. Gaining a sense of Agincourt's terrain will be crucial for our understanding of the unfolding shape of the battle.

Let us remember Agincourt's first ever battle tour, when in the summer of 1436 the Count of Richemont revisited the site with a few friends. Richemont – who had fought on the French side – now summed up the ground with brutal simplicity: 'it was too narrow'. This was indeed the key – the funnelling effect of the woods on either side of the villages of Agincourt and Tramecourt, allied with the terrible, clinging mud, was decisive. But it was only decisive because Henry V made the terrain work for him. It is usually said that the French made a disastrous choice of battleground. But the French were certainly not stupid and by drawing up their army across the Calais road, between Agincourt and Tramecourt, they attempted to direct proceedings to their best advantage. They were ready to fight a defensive battle and let the English come at them – the last thing that Henry and his tired and hungry army wanted to do. Henry then played the hand he was dealt with audacity and consummate skill.

The best way to understand this is to take a drive through the surrounding countryside, from Blangy to Ruisseauville, along the

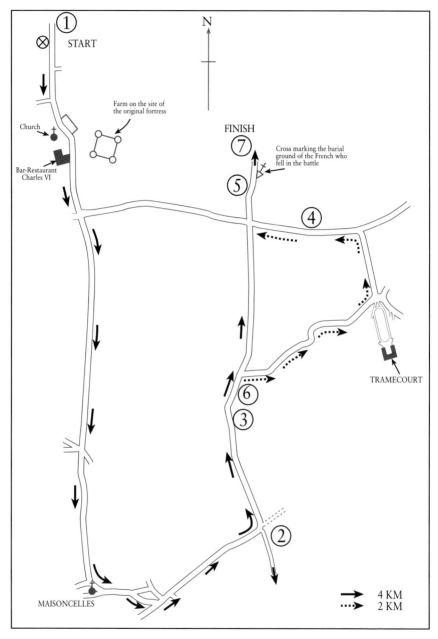

A tour of the battlefield and its seven vantage points. Use with the battle maps on pp. 101 and 111.

North of Agincourt the countryside opens out towards Ruisseauville. If the French had wanted to adopt an attacking plan of battle they would have blocked the Calais road here.

present D104. After crossing the Rriver Ternoise and passing through the little town of Blangy the road climbs steeply. It was from the ridge above the town that the English first saw the opposing army – and lined up ready to meet them on the afternoon of 24 October. The rolling countryside here gave the French an opportunity to fight a much more open, attacking battle, but they still preferred to fall back towards Agincourt. Continuing along the D104, we pass through the village of Maisoncelles, where the English set up camp that evening, and then reach the actual battlefield. The countryside then opens out again towards Ruisseauville, so the French had a further opportunity to fight an attacking battle on 25 October, by falling back in this direction, blocking the Calais road further north. They chose not to do so – and were willing, on the morning of battle, to wait for some two hours without advancing on the English position. Their choice of position between the woods of Agincourt and Tramecourt was thus a deliberate plan – to force Henry's exhausted army to attack their numerically superior force.

Open countryside north of Agincourt.

Henry, who had sent scouts to look over the battlefield, had to make the best use of the ground ahead. To follow this, I have selected seven 'vantage points' around the battlefield. These can be easily visited by car or by foot – and provide a backdrop to our developing story.

The Agincourt battlefield visitor's centre (1)

This is an ideal place to orientate oneself and is our first 'vantage point'. The modern battlefield centre is excellent: it gives a general overview of the battle — with a series of displays and film sequences – and puts it in overall context. One of its strengths is an emphasis on the hands-on realities of using medieval military equipment: the strength needed to pull a longbow; the confining and claustrophobic effect of armour. By trying to pull a weight representing the draw of a bow, or putting on a helmet and experiencing the huge limitations of vision and sound, one takes a step closer to Agincourt's combatants.

The longbow – the long yew bow used by England's archers – had a draw weight of well over 100 pounds and thus called for real strength and skill to be used properly. This weapon was very accurate in the hands of an expert — and also very powerful. A bow with a draw weight of 150 pounds could drive a heavy 60-gram arrow 230 yards, a lighter arrow 300 yards. A broadhead arrow – of

The Agincourt battlefield visitor centre.

the sort that might be used against horses – would break through mail with ease, while a narrow-pointed 'bodkin' shaft could be lethal even through plate armour.

These were the great strengths of the longbow. As Philippe Contamine rightly says in the battle centre's accompanying video, the English archers were 'an élite corps'. Their weakness was their vulnerability once hand-to-hand combat commenced. While the wealthiest bowmen might own a cheap armour breast plate – known as a 'brigandine' or 'jack' – or mail shirt, contemporary illustrations of warfare, which show most of the archers in armour, present an idealizsed picture. The reality was very different, for there was great diversity in archers' equipment and the vast majority had little, being 'without armour, dressed in their doublets, many without headgear', as Monstrelet remembered them before Agincourt.

Understanding this is crucial, for within the English army the archers needed to be properly protected to be really effective. Henry had to take advantage of any features of the terrain to achieve this and we know that at Agincourt he used the woods on either side of the battlefield, putting the majority of his archers there, on the flanks of his army. The dangers of leaving the archers exposed were shown in a fourteenth-century battle – at Mauron in Brittany in 1352. The English commander, Sir Walter Bentley, was outnumbered by the French and the battle site was unpromising, 'upon the open fields, without woods, ditches or other defences'. The French cavalry was able to break into the archers' position, killing many of them and creating a panic. Bentley managed to counter-attack and win the victory, but in the battle's aftermath he 'ordered thirty of the archers to be beheaded, because at the height of the battle, frightened by the numbers of the French, they had fled'. This grim piece of military discipline warns us that, in order to fight against the odds, the cohesion of the army was vital: everyone had to hold together.

The English camp at Maisoncelles (2)
Walking or driving out of Agincourt, we take the road to the south-east, quickly reaching the small village of Maisoncelles. Here we turn left, coming to the place where Henry and his army camped the night before battle. Our second 'vantage point' is the map and

The monument at Maisoncelles.

marker display of the battle, set out by the roadside at the intersection with the D104. From here the ground rises, although a clear view of the battlefield is not yet possible. But Henry had already learnt the lie of the land from his scouts.

The English war camp contained a mass of wagons. Commanding a relatively small force, Henry needed to fight with maximum economy, using everything at hand, including his baggage train. At dusk a French cavalry force had attacked a surprised group of English archers and the vigour of their action warned Henry that on the day of battle French horsemen might ride around the English position – skirting the far side of the woods – and attack his army from the rear. So his baggage train needed to be brought up to his battle line to act as a defensive shield. The chaplain said that on the morning of battle the king ordered his wagons to close up behind his army. Henry was too short of men to spare a proper reserve, so the baggage train could only be held by a scratch force of pages and a few archers. The danger was primarily from the French mounted combatants in their third line. These men could easily ride round the battlefield – such an enveloping manoeuvre had been seen at a recent battle, at Othée in 1408, when the Burgundian commander John the Fearless sent a force of several hundred horsemen around his opponents' position to attack them from behind. It was also

The English start position, viewed from the direction of Maisoncelles. The funnel effect of the woods is clearly visible.

envisaged in Marshal Boucicaut's original plan for Agincourt: a force of 200 picked cavalry would perform the task and if they met a defence line of carts they would attempt to break through it.

The importance of the wagon train raises fresh questions about the traditional account of the battle. If Henry advanced a further 700 yards, in knee-deep clinging mud, to get close to the enemy, did his wagons follow him and manoeuvre into a new position? If they did, it would make the advance even more cumbersome and time consuming. If they did not, it left the English vulnerable for the French cavalry might well break through the wagons, reform, and then charge the army from behind. In this scenario the terrain, far from helping the English, acts as a trap – allowing their force to be surrounded and annihilated.

The English start position (3)
Following the D104 for about 600 yards in the direction of Ruisseauville we come to the English start position, our third 'vantage point', beyond the top of a slight rise in the ground, with the battlefield now fully visible. On the left is the village of Agincourt, on the right that of Tramecourt, and with woods on both sides of the battlefield.

The English start position, as seen from the Agincourt-Tramecourt road (about 600 yards further north). The English position spanned the lines of trees to the left and right.

One body of archers was on the flank of the English army, on the edge of the Tramecourt woods, here seen on the left.

Henry now had to draw up his battle line, forging units of archers and men-at-arms into a coherent whole. The sources are not easy to interpret, for the chaplain described the king placing 'wedges' of archers in between the line of men-at-arms while Jean Le Fèvre and Jean de Waurin tell how Henry instructed Sir Thomas Erpingham 'to draw up his archers and put them in front in two wings'. Military historian Matthew Bennett has suggested a convincing compromise: the archers were mainly on the flanks – but some were also standing behind the men-at-arms in battle, ready to fall back just before the enemy arrived.

Again, the key idea is protection. In their defensive position, the archers in the main English battle line could draw back once the French approached and be shielded by their men-at-arms; those on the flanks by the woods and their protective stakes. Titus Livius noted that the main bodies of archers had an additional safeguard: 'on the two flanks hedges and thorn bushes protected the army from assault by the enemy'. It would be psychologically very difficult for the archers to leave the security of such a well-defended position and start trekking across the battlefield, in open view of their

A second body of archers was on the other flank of the army, on the edge of the Agincourt woods, to the far left of the photograph.

The woods at Tramecourt. An ambush of 200 English archers was hidden here.

opponents. The bowmen would have to keep in line with their men-at-arms as they went forward – and this would further slow the advance, as they would frequently need to stop, regroup and then start moving again. I believe that such a manoeuvre exposed the English army to an unacceptable degree of risk.

The ambush (4)
We now move up the D104 to its intersection with the Agincourt–Tramecourt road, and take a right turn towards the woods of Tramecourt and our fourth 'vantage point'. We cannot identify exactly where the archer ambush was set up. Monstrelet said they gathered in a small meadow within the wood, within firing range of the French army. It can be seen, even today, that the woods offer an excellent protective screen. The archer ambush has often been dismissed because of the testimony of Jean Le Fèvre. Le Fèvre said that he had heard about the ambush, but when he questioned one of the English combatants about it, the story was categorically denied:

Another view of the Tramecourt woods where the archers were concealed.

it was certified as true *by a man of honour* who was there on that day in the company of the king that nothing like this happened. (My emphasis.)

The reference to the 'man of honour' is significant – because setting up an ambush before battle might have been regarded as an underhand tactic. The soldier Jean de Bueil addressed such a dilemma in his book *Le Jouvencel* (The Youth). De Bueil acknowledged that an honourable knight would not want to win battle through a ruse – but went on to emphasize that knowledge of such matters was essential if one was to be successful in war. It is fascinating to note that the importance of adhering to codes of conduct outweighed thinking 'outside the box', by acting unexpectedly and cleverly, which was not regarded as praiseworthy until much later. An English 'man of honour' may have found the setting up of an ambush unpalatable and thus difficult to admit to – but I suspect in this case that there is no smoke without fire.

The French start position (5)
We now retrace our steps to the road intersection and then go about fifty yards further north along the D104 – to what is likely to have been the French start position, at the wider end of the funnel of woods. Here the ground rises slightly, giving an excellent view of the English position. The French cavalry were on the wings; the crossbowmen and lightly armed combatants in the rear. The main strength of the army was in its dismounted men-at-arms. Here, as Titus Livius recalled, they were more than thirty men deep – against an English line just four men deep. These were daunting odds. The disparity between the men-at-arms of each side was far greater than at Crécy or Poitiers. Clifford Rogers has suggested to me that this was probably one reason for the division between Henry and his chief nobles at Harfleur on 5 October: 'Where his captains were willing to face 2 or 3:1 odds in men-at-arms they were not willing to face odds of 10:1. Henry had more faith in his archers than did his advisers'.

To counter, Henry needed to tire this large French force as much as possible, making it advance the full distance in the terrible mud, exposed to the withering fire of his archers. The French had no overall commander and the last-minute arrival of their high-ranking noblemen pitched the dukes of Orléans, Alençon and Bourbon

The French position at the wider end of the 'funnel'. The Agincourt woodland is on the left. The ground rises here, allowing an excellent view of the English position.

The French start position seen from the Agincourt-Tramecourt road. Agincourt's church is just visible.

alongside Marshal Boucicaut and the Constable D'Albret. Jean de Bueil had Agincourt in mind when he wrote that in battle having just one commander was essential. This is why the tactic of provocation was so important. All the leading French noblemen were in the front line and Henry knew this left no one to restrain their army if only he could goad it forward.

The limited English advance (6)

We now return along the D104 to our sixth 'vantage point', just ahead of the original English start position (3). I argue that, instead of a large-scale English advance of at least 700 yards, the English undertook a limited one of about twenty paces (the distance given by the Pseudo-Elmham). They then provoked the French into going forward, taunting them with a raucous hunting cry and, simultaneously, a shower of arrows from the archer ambush.

This way of reading the battle was suggested to me by an unusual challenge made by another English king – Edward IV –

The English made a limited advance, about 20 paces forward, to provoke the French into attacking. They taunted their opponents with a hunting cry, and the archers concealed in the Tramecourt woods opened fire on the French flank.

before his invasion of France in 1475, sixty years after Agincourt. A comparison with the Agincourt campaign was very much in participants' minds and one English soldier – John Albon – dashed off a letter at the very place on 27 July 1475, saying how the king, lords and army 'were at Agincourt this day' and speculating 'whether the French king will give him battle or not'. Edward IV's great-uncle, the duke of York, had perished at Agincourt and I believe that the king now taunted his adversary, Louis XI, with a reference to that momentous battle:

> We shall hunt through parts of France and there I will blow my horn and release my hounds.

He then made a deliberate allusion to his distinguished predecessor – the duke of York – and his hunting treatise, declaring emphatically: 'I am master of the game.'

I decided to look again at *The Master of the Game*, which York had dedicated to Henry V when he was still Prince of Wales. I was struck by French chroniclers' use of the hunting term 'huer' – the vocal imitation of the hunting horn – to describe the English cry, and believed it possible to build a convincing alternative scenario around it. My new reading of the battle allows Henry V to keep all the advantages of his defensive position and forces the French to do all the work. As we move back northwards along the D104 towards the Agincourt–Tramecourt road, we are witnessing the scene of the fiercest fighting.

The French Calvary (7)

We continue along the D104 past the intersection, and about 100 yards or so to the right is the French Calvary: the name now given to the memorial marking the site of one of the French burial pits. As we pause here, we can reflect on the terrible decision Henry had to make – killing French prisoners to prevent a fresh enemy attack on his exhausted men. There was a precedent for his action – at the battle of Aljubarotta in 1385 – when an Anglo-Portuguese army defeated their Castilian opponents. Froissart related how, at the end of the battle, elements of the Castilian vanguard regrouped and prepared for another assault. If fighting was resumed and some of the prisoners picked up weapons and joined in, the odds against the Anglo-Portuguese force would be too great, so the order was given

The Calvary. The cross marks the location of one of the French burial pits.

to put them to death. In the same way, Henry's order, although appalling to us, was necessary to save his army.

Standing by the Calvary, we can recall the casualties suffered by the opposing armies. The disparity between the two sides is astounding. The French buried dead in their thousands. Titus Livius and the Pseudo-Elmham put the English figure at about a hundred; other sources reckoned it even smaller. Thomas Elmham, after noting the deaths of the duke of York and the earl of Suffolk, added that 'scarcely thirty other English fell by the sword' and Shakespeare then recorded these figures accurately, with 10,000 French slain and the English dead 'but five and twenty'. These figures are hard for us to credit, and for an audience in wartime Britain – facing terrible losses of fighting men – they were utterly unbelievable. So when Olivier brought out his film, in 1944, he altered the text to increase the numbers of English dead, putting the count at 'five and twenty *score*' (my emphasis).

Shakespeare was closer to the truth when he portrayed the tiny number of English casualties as a kind of miracle. 'Oh God' declared Henry 'thy arm was here'. Many of the French had been asphyxiated in the terrible crush of the battlefield. Yet as well as suffering misfortune and the consequences of bad judgement, the French were also confronted by an English army fighting with extraordinary power. As the battle unfolded, Henry's army gained in certainty and courage until his men felt themselves almost invincible, something their shattered opponents sensed all too well. At its end, Thomas Basin recorded ruefully, one Englishman could chase off ten terrified Frenchmen.

Medieval commanders sometimes dedicated a battle to God in a token act of piety. But Henry's reverence was real. In the victory celebrations in London on 23 November 1415, the chaplain related:

> from his quiet demeanour, gentle pace and solemn progress it might have been gathered that the king, silently pondering the matter in his heart, was rendering thanks to God alone, not man.

In 1475, when another English king – Edward IV – was about to invade France, he was presented with an encouraging book of martial deeds. *The Book of Noblesse* was drawn from the reminiscences of Sir John Fastolf and other veterans of the Agincourt campaign. Its author, William Worcester, spoke of the right way to prepare for combat, how soldiers should not become preoccupied with thoughts of material gain but instead let God show his 'power and fortune'. Worcester added: 'I have been credibly informed that Henry V used the same counsel amongst his army.'

I have argued throughout that Agincourt was indeed a heroic triumph of the underdog. The story has not been recorded in this way simply as a clever piece of propaganda. It reflects a genuine and powerful truth. This victory against the odds was how Henry and his troops actually experienced the battle. *The Book of Noblesse* puts the soldiers' view simply and directly: Henry V 'with a few number' had resoundingly beaten the French. In the margin was the annotation: 'victory does not lie in a great multitude of people'.

Here is the real story of Agincourt, and a testimony to Henry's inspirational leadership and the courage and unity of his army. After his annotation the author added simply – 'nota bene'. We should do well to follow suit.

Further Reading

Allmand, Christopher, *The Hundred Years War* (Cambridge University Press, 1988).
— *Henry V* (Yale University Press, 1997).
Ayton, Andrew, and Sir Philip Preston, *The Battle of Crécy, 1346* (Boydell, 2005).
Bennett, Matthew, *Agincourt 1415: Triumph Against the Odds* (Osprey, 1991).
Burne, Alfred, *The Agincourt War* (Greenhill Books, 1991).
Anne Curry, *The Battle of Agincourt: Sources and Interpretations* (Boydell & Brewer, 2000).
— *Agincourt: A New History* (Tempus, 2005).
Dockray, Keith, *Henry V* (Tempus, 2004).
Goodman, Anthony, *The Wars of the Roses: The Soldiers' Experience* (Tempus, 2005).
Hewitt, H J, *The Black Prince's Expedition of 1355–1357* (Pen & Sword Books, 2004).
Hibbert, Christopher, *Agincourt* (Windrush Press, 1995).
Keegan, Sir John, *The Face of Battle* (Pimlico, 1991).
Mercer, Malcolm, *Henry V: The Rebirth of Chivalry* (National Archives, 2004).
Prestwich, Michael, *Armies and Warfare in the Middle Ages: The English Experience* (Yale University Press, 1999).
— *Edward I* (Yale University Press, 1997).
Rogers, Clifford, *War, Cruel and Sharp: English Strategy under Edward III, 1327–1360* (Boydell & Brewer, 2000).
Strickland, Matthew, and Robert Hardy, *The Great Warbow* (Sutton, 2005).

Notes

Chapter 1: Rediscovering Agincourt

This chapter explores ideas on the psychology of battle – the state of mind of the combatants – first set out by J F Verbruggen. His original 1954 study has now been revised and translated: J F Verbruggen, *The Art of Warfare in Western Europe during the Middle Ages*, tr. S Willard and R W Southern (Boydell & Brewer, 1997). Henry's chaplain remembered the king citing the example of Judas Maccabeus before battle. This detail seems authentic and allows us to see where medieval commanders might find inspiration. Maccabeus was also a significant model for two of Henry's warrior predecessors. Edward I commissioned murals of his life for the Painted Chamber in the Palace of Westminster; Edward III was described on his tomb as 'a strong Maccabeus in wars'. I have benefited here from Jenni Nuttall's article, ' "Vostre Humble Matatyas": Culture, Politics and the Percys', in Linda Clark (ed.), *The Fifteenth Century*, vol. 5 (Boydell & Brewer, 2005). For information on the making of Olivier's *Henry V* I am grateful to Geoffrey Wheeler and Richard Olivier.

Chapter 2: A King Goes to War

The focus here is on Henry V as a commander – showing how he cared for his troops. The details on John Bradmore and the operation after Shrewsbury are taken from Strickland and Hardy, *The Great Warbow* (Sutton, 2005), pp. 284–5, and Carole Rawcliffe, 'Master Surgeons at the Lancastrian Court', in Jenny Stratford (ed.), *The Lancastrian Court* (Donnington, 2003). Henry's comment on the battle at Grosmont, in 1405, is found in Charles Kingsford, *Henry V: The Typical Medieval Hero* (London, 1901), pp. 51–2. For a sample of John Bromyard's writing see Christopher Allmand (ed.), *Society at*

War: the Experience of England and France during the Hundred Years War (Boydell, 1973), pp. 38–9. John Cheney's letter is in Sir Harris Nicolas, *History of the Battle of Agincourt* (London, 1832), appendix, p. 66; further biographical detail in J S Roskell, L Clark and C Rawcliffe (eds), *The Commons 1386–1422*, 4 vols (Sutton, 1992), vol. 2, pp. 552–4. Material on the surgeon Thomas Morstede has kindly been provided by Professor Carole Rawcliffe. She comments ('Master Surgeons', p. 209) on Henry's medical train: 'No such arrangements seem to have been made for English armies before 1415'. The references to Mowbray and St George are from Rowena Archer's 1984 Oxford DPhil thesis, 'The Mowbrays, Earls of Nottingham and Dukes of Norfolk, to 1432'. Strickland's petition is in Curry, *Sources*, p. 450; for his courage at Shrewsbury, *Calendar of Patent Rolls*, 1401–5, pp. 304, 468.

Chapter 3: Once More unto the Breach
I believe Henry V deserves high praise for the way he conducted the siege of Harfleur. His grandfather, John of Gaunt, had failed to reduce the town during his 1369 expedition – French sources said that Gaunt attacked hard but the fortifications were too strong: James Sherborne, 'John of Gaunt, Edward III's Retinue and the French Campaign of 1369', in R A Griffiths and J Sherborne (eds), *Kings and Nobles in the Later Middle Ages* (Sutton, 1986). Henry's use of artillery was all-important: see Bert S Hall, *Warfare and Weapons in Renaissance Europe* (Baltimore, 1997) – kindly drawn to my attention by Dr David Grummitt. Fastolf's experience at Harfleur is in *English Suits Before the Parlement of Paris, 1420–1436*, ed. C T Allmand and C A J Armstrong (London, 1982), p. 264. On the medical provision for Henry's soldiers see G E Gask, 'The Medical Services of Henry V's Campaign on the Somme, 1415', *Proceedings of the Royal Society of Medicine*, 16 (1922) and Rowena Archer's DPhil thesis, cited above.

Chapter 4: On the March
This chapter, which argues that Henry sought to face the French in battle, has benefited considerably from Clifford Rogers, 'Henry V's Military Strategy in 1415', in L J Andrew Villalon and Donald J Kagay (eds), *The Hundred Years War: A Wider Focus*, vol. 1 (Brill, 2004), pp. 399–427. I have stressed the importance of the Oriflamme – a symbol to rally French support – in BBC Radio 4's *In Our Time* and Channel 4's *Agincourt*, both in September 2004. Bardolf's letter

is in Curry, *Sources*, pp. 446–7; Hostell's petition: ibid., pp. 449–50. The material on John Feriby is from History of Parliament Trust, London, unpublished article on John Feriby for the 1422–1509 section by Linda Clark. I am grateful to the History of Parliament Trust for allowing me to see this article in draft. For John Bromley at Corbie we rely on a sixteenth-century source and Anne Curry, *Agincourt: A New History* (Tempus, 2005), p. 147, is sceptical that incident ever took place. However, I find the description of Bromley's martial endeavour quite plausible. As Matthew Bennett remarked (*Agincourt: Triumph Against the Odds*, pp. 50–1) 'it was the kind of the thing that happened in the countless small skirmishes of medieval warfare', adding that 'the king's response in this situation was typical of his grasp of military psychology'.

Chapter 5: The Battle

For the battle itself, I have found Clifford Roger's article, 'The Battle of Agincourt', in Villalon and Kagay (eds), *The Hundred Years War*, vol. 2 (Brill, forthcoming, 2006) and Strickland and Hardy, *The Great Warbow* (Sutton, 2005), pp. 318–38, particularly useful. I have considered ritual preparation of an army for combat in 'The Battle of Verneuil (17 August 1424): Towards a History of Courage', *War in History*, 9 (2002), 375–411, and *Bosworth 1485: Psychology of a Battle* (Tempus, 2002). For an accessible, modern translation of Vegetius see N P Milner, *Vegetius: Epitome of Military Science* (Liverpool University Press, 1996). The duke of Brabant's last-minute arrival at the battlefield is related in Dynter's Chronicle (Curry, *Sources*, pp. 172-5); Bertrand de Blois's rush to the site is in the Archives Communales of Amiens, CC16, fo. 40. On the archers' stakes see Matthew Bennett, 'The Development of Battle Tactics in the Hundred Years War', in A Curry and M Hughes (eds), *Arms, Armies and Fortifications in the Hundred Years War* (Boydell, 1994), pp. 15-16, and Rowena Archer's important review article 'Agincourt, Agincourt! Know ye not Agincourt?', in *The Ricardian* (2004). On the hunting cry and a possible reinterpretation of Erpingham's command: Strickland and Hardy, *The Great Warbow*, pp. 142–4, and for background, J G Cummings, *The Hound and the Hawk: The Art of Medieval Hunting* (London, 1988).

Chapter 6: The Legacy

The reconstruction of the battle of Verneuil is derived from my *War in History* (2002) article – cited above – and featured on Channel 4's

Weapons that Made Britain – Armour in August 2004. For the captivity of Charles duke of Orléans see my ' "Gardez Mon Corps, Sauvez Ma Terre" – Immunity from War and the Lands of a Captive Knight: The Siege of Orléans (1428–9) Revisited', in Mary-Jo Arn (ed.), *Charles d'Orléans in England* (Boydell, 2000); and for a later English martial achievement, 'The Relief of Avranches (1439): An English Feat of Arms at the End of the Hundred Years War', in N. Rogers (ed.), *England in the Fifteenth Century* (Paul Watkins, 1994). Sir William Bourchier's war career is from *The Commons 1386–1422.*, vol. 2, pp. 315–17, and material supplied by Professor Carole Rawcliffe. The Calais garrison's observance of the Agincourt anniversary is in David Grummitt, 'Calais and the Crown', in D. Grummitt (ed.), *The English Experience in France, c.1450–1558* (Ashgate, 2002), p. 54. For the continuing power of Shakespeare's *Henry V*: Emma Smith, *Shakespeare in Production: King Henry V* (Cambridge University Press, 2002).

Chapter 7: The Battlefield Today
The modern battlefield centre is at 24 Rue Charles VI, Azincourt. Background material to this chapter has been supplied by Clifford Rogers and Matthew Strickland. For Edward IV's hunting challenge to Louis XI in 1475, John Albon's letter and the importance of *The Book of Noblesse* see Colin Richmond, '1485 and All That, or What was Going on at the Battle of Bosworth', in P W Hammond (ed.), *Richard III: Loyalty, Lordship and Law* (London, 2000). The references are from *The Boke of Noblesse*, ed. J G Nichols (reprinted New York, 1972), pp. 28, 31–2.

Illustrations
Maps, still photographs and other illustrations supplied by Geoffrey Wheeler; modern photographs of the battlefield by the author. Illustrations on pp. 76, 98 and 117 provided by C.E.J. Smith.

Index

Page numbers in italics refer to illustrations.